STUDY GUIDE FOR

BASIC STATISTICS

TALES OF DISTRIBUTIONS

4TH EDITION

STUDY GUIDE FOR

BASIC STATISTICS

TALES OF DISTRIBUTIONS

4TH EDITION

CHRIS SPATZ
Hendrix College

JAMES O. JOHNSTON
Oglala Lakota College, Retired

BROOKS/COLE PUBLISHING COMPANY
Pacific Grove, California

MAI 338/1987

Brooks/Cole Publishing Company
A Division of Wadsworth, Inc.

Printed in the United States of America

10 9 8 7 6 5 4 3 2

ISBN 0-534-09488-0

Sponsoring Editor: Phil Curson
Consulting Editor: Roger Kirk
Senior Assistant: Amy Mayfield
Production Editor: Nancy Shammas
Cover Design: Kelly Shoemaker
Word Processing: Bob Lande
Art Coordinator: Sue C. Howard

Preface

This study guide is designed to accompany the fourth edition of <u>Basic Statistics: Tales of Distributions</u>. Each chapter begins with a one- to two-page summary of the major points in the corresponding chapter of the textbook. Additional explanations are given for the concepts that our students have trouble with. The problems that follow are divided into three groups: (1) multiple-choice questions (about 12–16 per chapter); (2) short-answer or interpretation questions; and (3) problems. The multiple-choice questions emphasize the concepts of the chapter and are considered somewhat difficult by our students. The short-answer questions range from simple listing to composing a short essay. The interpretation questions describe an experiment and its statistical analysis; the task is to tell the story in words. The problems are designed to give practice on several things--choosing the right statistical test, applying formulas and doing the arithmetic, and interpreting the results using the terms of the problem. Many of these problems are modeled after published research. We chose these problems because they were either classical studies or recent, interesting studies. The answers to all problems will be found at the back of the study guide.

It is a pleasure to acknowledge the assistance of students at Hendrix College who worked many of these problems and made comments. The staff at Brooks/Cole did its usual good job of converting a manuscript into an attractive book.

Chris Spatz
James O. Johnston

Contents

CHAPTER 1 INTRODUCTION

SUMMARY

The overall purpose of the first chapter of the textbook is to introduce to you

1. some broad categories used in statistics (for example, descriptive and inferential statistics and experimental design),
2. some important terms and concepts (for example, parameter, independent variable, and lower limit),
3. the organization of the book.

In addition we illustrate the place that statistics occupies in the field of epistemology and the variety of disciplines that use statistics. We also emphasize the fact that you will learn more and become more persuasive if you take an active approach in your studies.

We think the kind of reasoning people use when they do statistics problems can be applied to many other situations that aren't the least bit statistical. Because of the general applicability of statistical reasoning, it is a good investment for you to devote some of your best efforts to this course.

The notion of <u>descriptive statistics</u> is pretty simple and straightforward: a single number or name that is used to capture a particular characteristic of a set of data. <u>Inferential statistics</u> is a set of procedures that allows you to make a decision about a population even though all your information comes from a sample, which is recognized as being influenced by chance. (To get a more thorough understanding of inferential statistics, you might peek ahead to the first part of Chapter 7.)

The idea of using a <u>sample</u> as a substitute for a larger, unmeasurable <u>population</u> will be found in every chapter that follows. The characteristics of samples, <u>statistics</u>, and the characteristics of populations, <u>parameters</u>, are not usually confused. The two p's go together and the two s's go together.

Quantitative and qualitative variables find their way into the text in several chapters after this first one. Quantitative variables have <u>lower</u> and <u>upper limits</u> and are expressed in amounts. Qualitative variables have names and are expressed as kinds.

Scales of measurement (nominal, ordinal, interval, and ratio) have precise definitions. On a <u>ratio</u> scale a zero means that none of the variable being measured is there. An <u>interval</u> scale's zero is just a convenient amount of the variable being measured. Like the ratio scale, however, equal distances on the scale represent equal amounts of the variable. An <u>ordinal</u> scale indicates greater-than and less-than, but equal distances between numbers do not represent equal amounts of the thing being measured. Finally, on a <u>nominal</u> scale different numbers do not even mean greater-than or less-than; they simply mean that the two things being assessed are different.

If you know the topic of <u>experimental design</u>, you can plan the procedures necessary to gather data. If you know the topic of <u>statistics</u>, you can analyze the data. A good experimentalist should be competent in both topics. So, when we considered including in the text a particular sidelight on experimental design, we nearly always decided to put it in. As a consequence, the distinctions among <u>independent</u>, <u>dependent</u>, and <u>extraneous variables</u>, which are troublesome for some students, will appear again and again. Do all the study guide problems that ask you to make these distinctions.

In the section on "Statistics and Philosophy," we defined epistemology as the study of knowledge. Some knowledge is created by using reason; one example of a technique based on reason is statistics.

A 200-year history of statistics concentrates on the beginnings of institutions and the beginnings of statistics courses. Four levels of competence in statistics are described.

The textbook describes itself and its features. We want to reemphasize the objectives at the beginning of each chapter and the three glossaries.

Finally, we expect that you will spend several hours with this study guide. If so, you will find that you will want to refer to it in the future after you have finished this course. We hope that this study guide, too, becomes part of your personal library.

MULTIPLE-CHOICE QUESTIONS

1. The purposes of inferential statistics is to

   (1) select representative samples;
   (2) make decisions about populations;
   (3) characterize a set of data with one number or name;
   (4) all of the above.

2. The Zeigarnik effect

   (1) is the distinction between statistics and experimental design;
   (2) is that numbers mean different things depending on the scale of measurement;
   (3) is a phenomenon of memory;
   (4) all of the above.

3. The techniques of statistics are used in

   (1) psychology and education, at present;
   (2) answer (1) plus Biology;
   (3) disciplines in the social sciences, plus biology;
   (4) a wide variety of disciplines.

4.   _____ are used as estimates of parameters.

    (1)   statistics;
    (2)   constants;
    (3)   populations;
    (4)   upper limits.

5.   Five means more than three on the

    (1)   ordinal scale;
    (2)   interval scale;
    (3)   ratio scale;
    (4)   all of the above.

6.   Many schools rank their graduates each year
      from highest to lowest. Graduates wind up
      with scores like 14 and 131. Such a scale
      is one example of a(n) _____ scale.

    (1)   nominal;
    (2)   ordinal;
    (3)   interval;
    (4)   ratio.

7.   On the _____ scale, zero means a complete
      absence of the thing measured.

    (1)   ordinal;
    (2)   interval;
    (3)   ratio;
    (4)   all of the above.

8.   Epistemology deals with the nature of

    (1)   reason;
    (2)   experience;
    (3)   mathematics;
    (4)   knowledge.

9.   In a study of the effect of handedness on
      athletic ability, subjects were divided
      into three groups--right-handed, left-
      handed, and ambidextrous. Athletic ability
      was measured on a 12-point scale. The num-
      ber of levels of the independent variable
      in this experiment is

(1) twelve;
(2) four;
(3) three;
(4) two.

10. In the study of handedness and athletic ability, the dependent variable is

(1) handedness;
(2) athletic ability;
(3) not described;
(4) both (1) and (2).

11. The independent variable is to the dependent variable as the

(1) sidewalk is to the street;
(2) street is to the sidewalk;
(3) germ is to the disease;
(4) disease is to the germ.

12. If an experiment has two groups of subjects and if both groups are "chronic schizophrenics," then chronic schizophrenia is most likely a(n)

(1) independent variable;
(2) dependent variable;
(3) controlled extraneous variable;
(4) any of the above are likely.

13. In an experiment to determine the effect of amounts of insecticide on tomato production, an extraneous variable would be

(1) the amount of insecticide;
(2) the amount of production;
(3) both (1) and (2);
(4) neither (1) nor (2).

14. In an experiment on the effect of sleep on memory, the independent variable might be

(1) number of hours of sleep;
(2) recall score on a test;

(3) gender of the subjects;
(4) gender of the experimenter.

SHORT-ANSWER QUESTIONS

Distinguish between

1. descriptive and inferential statistics;

2. populations and samples;

3. interval and ordinal scales of measurement.

PROBLEMS

1. For each of the following studies, identify

   a. the independent variable,
   b. the dependent variable,
   c. a controlled extraneous variable,
   d. a population of interest,
   e. a sample,
   f. a statistic that would be computed,
   g. a parameter that would be estimated,
   h. a variable measured with a nominal scale, and
   i. another variable and the scale used to measure it.

   Write a sentence that tells what the study found.

   A. The paper towel market had become saturated with competing products. The manufacturer of SOPPO towels decided to take a swipe at his competitors and wipe away his company's messy financial problems by releasing a "new, improved" version of SOPPO towels. To prove that SOPPO towels absorb more mess faster than either SLURPY or GRUNGE GATHERER towels (the leading competitors), an "experiment" was conducted and videotaped. A full roll of each brand of towel was placed in a vat containing two gallons of raspberry punch (one of your more common household messmakers). After 30 seconds, stopcocks at the bottom of the three vats were opened and the unabsorbed punch drained into beakers. The amount of punch drained off was measured, "proving unequivocally" (said the narrator) that SOPPO absorbed more of the punch in 30 seconds than did its two leading competitors.

B. This is a study based on an article by Wender and Klein (1981). At a psychiatric hospital, a group of patients diagnosed as depressed was compared to another group that was classified as manic. All patients had been admitted to the hospital within the previous week. An analysis of each individual's biogenic amine neurotransmitters (brain chemicals involved in nerve firing), showed that the depressed patients scored low and the manic patients scored high.

C. An educational researcher interested in the relative effectiveness of individual and group problem-solving techniques invited 20 randomly selected high school seniors from each of the two high schools in town to a meeting. She discussed with the entire group the negative consequences of the existing rivalry between the two schools and the positive consequences that could result from cooperation. She then explained to them the brainstorming technique of problem solving--thinking of as many solutions as possible without regard to quality or practicability of the solutions. The 40 students were randomly divided into two groups of 20. One group brainstormed the problem for an hour as individuals, writing down as many solutions as possible. The others were assigned to four groups of five students each. Each group brainstormed the problem for an hour, with one student in each group writing down the solutions as the group generated them. The experimenter counted the number of different solutions generated by individuals and the number generated by groups. More solutions were generated by individuals.

D. Gestalt psychologists showed that people organize their perceptions according to certain principles, one of which they called closure. Closure is a tendency to subjectively close gaps-- to perceptually complete uncompleted figures, memories, concepts, and so on. A pair of experimenters (Calhoun & Johnston, 1968) wanted to know if this tendency for closure was stronger in high-anxiety people than in low-anxiety people. They administered the Taylor Manifest Anxiety Scale to 381 introductory psychology students. After eliminating subjects with less than normal vision, the 21 lowest-anxiety and 21 highest-anxiety students were shown a chart containing 33 fine-line circles, six of which were closed. The rest had a small gap at the top, bottom, right, or left. Subjects were instructed to say where the gap was or that it was a closed circle. The number of errors was recorded for each subject. The high-anxiety group made significantly more errors.

2. What are the lower and upper limits of the following numbers?

a. 4.3 minutes
b. 6 errors
c. 56.75°C

d. $45.50
e. 49 grams

3. The following pairs represent the lower and upper limits of what numbers?

   a. 4.5–5.5
   b. 6.35–6.45
   c. .815–.825
   d. 0.5–1.5
   e. 652.35–652.45

4. Describe each of the following statements as descriptive (D) or inferential (I).

   _____a. This is the year our football team will win the conference!
   _____b. That would be nice, but we graduated Bubonski, remember? He led the conference in rushing last year.
   _____c. Yeah, but we got a new guy who's gonna be even better. I watched him practice yesterday. He's gonna be great.
   _____d. Well, I hope you're right, but I'll be satisfied if we just have a winning season.

5. Describe each of the following statements as descriptive (D) or inferential (I).

   _____a. Every student I've talked to is angry about the big tuition increase, so I wouldn't be surprised if a lot of students transferred out next term.
   _____b. Enrollment is already down by 5%.
   _____c. Well, last spring's graduating high school senior classes in this area were down 10%, too, so there isn't as big a crop of freshmen.
   _____d. That could account for some of the enrollment drop, but this college usually draws over half its

students from outside this area.
It should still be doing that.

6. Identify each measurement below as being based on a quantitative or qualitative variable. For quantitative variables identify the lower and upper limits of the measurement.

	Kind of Variable	Limits
a. 414, dollars received from a part-time job	_____	_____
b. 16, cubic yards of dirt	_____	_____
c. 8, identification for Druid College among private schools in Transylvania	_____	_____
d. 3.0, millions of dollars in the budget	_____	_____
e. 101.9, km/hr registered on a radar machine used by the state police	_____	_____
f. 23.95, the time in seconds required for Sam to swim 50 yards	_____	_____

7. Identify the quantitative variables below by writing in lower and upper limits of each score. Write qualitative beside the variables that deserve such a name.

a. 2 styles of sonnets   _____
b. 3 feet of paper   _____
c. 4 species of protozoans   _____
d. 5.0 seconds of time   _____
e. 6.05 grains of gold   _____
f. 7.95 decibels of noise   _____
g. 100 points on an IQ test   _____

8. A classic experiment by Warden (1931) measured the motivation of rats for food,

water, or sex. After deprivation, a rat
had to cross an electrified grid to get to
the goal object. (The whole apparatus was
called the Columbia Obstruction Box.) The
amount of electrical shock a rat would
tolerate and still cross was measured.
(Thirst came out as the strongest motive.)
Name the dependent and independent variable. Identify an extraneous variable that
should have been controlled.

9. The importance of early psychic traumas of
children as a precursor of cancer has been
investigated. Psychic traumas were those
in which emotional relationships brought
pain and desertion. Of 450 cancer
patients, 72% had experienced such an early
psychic trauma. Only 10% of a noncancerous
control group reported such an experience.
Name the independent variable and dependent
variables and at least one extraneous
variable that should have been controlled.

CHAPTER 2 THE ORGANIZATION OF DATA, GRAPHS, AND CENTRAL VALUES

SUMMARY

If you understand the material in this chapter you can take a set of measurements, organize them into an appropriate frequency distribution (either simple or grouped), construct a graph, identify the direction of skew (if any), and calculate and describe all appropriate measures of central value. Except for finding the mean of a set of means, the previous sentence summarizes your tasks in Chapter 2.

This chapter started with unorganized data (chaos) and proceeded to more and more precise methods of description. The unorganized data were reduced to a simple frequency distribution, which was then further reduced to a grouped frequency distribution. Graphs are a different (and sometimes superior) way to present frequency distributions and other relationships.

Establishing class intervals is occasionally troublesome for some students. After establishing i, write the lowest class interval at the bottom of your workspace. Make certain that the lower limit is a multiple of i. Add higher class intervals until you reach the upper limit of the highest class interval, which, if your spacing plans have been good, will be near the top of your workspace.

You learned three methods of describing a set of data with one number or word. Of the three, the median gives students the most trouble. Calculating the median involves more steps than either the mean or the mode. The path that leads to calculating the median correctly is a path full of practice. If you make errors, reread the section of your text that includes the list of steps, and study Figure 2.11.

   The two mathematical characteristics of the mean will be referred to in later chapters. If you do not feel that you understand the expressions, $\Sigma(X - X) = 0$ and $\Sigma(X - X)^2$ is a minimum, you should make up a small set of data and carry out the operations that the formulas describe. If this is not sufficient, ask someone else for help.

   The distinctions made in Chapter 1 among nominal, ordinal, interval, and radio data are important for the graphs and central values in Chapter 2. Nominal data call for a bar graph and a mode.

   Calculating a mean of a set of means is easy. Recognizing when you can work from the individual means and when you have to go back to an overall sum of X takes some practice. We provide some in the problems that follow.

MULTIPLE-CHOICE QUESTIONS

   1.   In a set of scores that ranged from 11 to 50, an acceptable lowest class interval would be

        (1)   11–13;
        (2)   11–14;
        (3)   9–12;
        (4)   9–11.

   2.   To present a frequency distribution of nominal data you should use

        (1)   a polygon;
        (2)   a bar graph;
        (3)   a histogram;
        (4)   a line graph.

   3.   Which of the following is not used to present a frequency distribution?

        (1)   bar graph;
        (2)   histogram;

(3)   frequency polygon;
✓ (4)   line graph.

4.   The U.S. Department of Agriculture reported the total number of bushels harvested of corn, soy beans, wheat, rice, and oats. This is a frequency distribution of a

✓ (1)   nominal variable;
(2)   ordinal variable;
(3)   interval variable;
(4)   ratio variable.

5.   When the bar graph showing college majors was presented in your text, the convention that was violated was that of

(1)   the number of class intervals;
(2)   the size of the class intervals;
(3)   both of the above;
✓ (4)   placing frequency on the Y axis.

6.   The fact that the middle of a series of items is more difficult to learn than the beginning or the end is known as the

(1)   series effect;
(2)   middling effect;
(3)   bimodal effect;
✓ (4)   serial position effect.

7.   A frequency distribution with a mean of 100 and a median of 90 is

✓ (1)   positively skewed;
(2)   negatively skewed;
(3)   neither positive nor negative;
(4)   cannot be determined from the information given.

8.   Suppose a frequency distribution with a range of 0 to 100 was positively skewed. The greatest frequency of scores would be clustered around

✓ (1) 0;
  (2) 50;
  (3) 100;
  (4) unknown, not enough information is given.

9. Which of the following words could legitimately fit into this sentence: "That simple frequency distribution has two _____, 13 and 18."

  (1) means;
  (2) medians;
  (3) modes;
  (4) all of the above.

10. The appropriate statistic for conveying the central value of a nominal variable is

  (1) mean;
  (2) median;
  ✓(3) mode;
  (4) any of the three above, but the mean is preferable.

11. Your text noted which of the following as a characteristic of the mean?

  (1) The sum of the results of squaring the difference between each score and the mean is a minimum;
  ✓ (2) The sum of the results of squaring the difference between each score and the mean is zero;
  (3) Both of the above;
  (4) Neither of the above.

12. In which situation below would the mean be an appropriate measure of central value?

  (1) Most of the scores are near the minimum, a few are in the middle range, and there are almost none near the maximum;
  (2) We have frequency data on cows, horses, mules, and goats;

15

    (3) The data categories in the soil analy-
         sis are: 0−2 ppm, 3−5 ppm, 6−8 ppm,
         9−11 ppm, and over 11 ppm;
 ✓ (4) None of the above.

13. "For our study of driving habits, we
     recorded the speed of every fifth vehicle
     on Drury Lane. Nearly every car traveled
     right at the speed limit or a little over,
     but there were some that were 10 mph under,
     even fewer at 20 mph under, and one car
     that crept by at just 15 mph. On the basis
     of the central value of our data, we drew
     conclusions about all drivers on this
     stretch of road." The proper central value
     calculated from the data is the

     (1) population median;
 ✓ (2) sample median;
     (3) population mean (μ);
     (4) sample mean ($\overline{X}$).

14. Two investigators tested their friends for
     memory span. The first tested five people
     and found a mean of 6.0. The second tested
     nine people and found a mean of 7.0. The
     overall mean for the data gathered is

     (1) 6.00;
     (2) 6.50;
 ✓ (3) 6.64;
     (4) 7.00.

SHORT-ANSWER QUESTIONS

 1. Your textbook described three situations in
     which the median should be used rather than
     the mean. List them.

 2. In three sentences, distinguish among the
     frequency polygon, the histogram, and the
     bar graph.

 3. "Our company has three divisions. Based on
     our capital invested, Division A made $.10

per dollar, Division B made $.20 per dollar, and Division C made $.25 per dollar. Therefore, the profit for the company was $.1833 per dollar invested." Do you agree with this conclusion? Explain why you agree or disagree.

4. This is a think question about the distribution of class size in a typical college. There are usually a few courses, typically at the freshman level, that have large enrollments. Most of the courses, however, are at the junior and senior level, and in these courses enrollments are much smaller. Suppose the mean class size in such a college was 23. Would the median be larger or smaller?

5. For each situation, decide which of the four types of graph would be most appropriate. After your answer, write your reason.

   a. a telephone poll of 100 houses to determine what TV show the person was watching;
   b. a telephone poll of 100 houses to determine household income;
   c. mean number of hospital admissions for each day of the week in New York City;
   d. attendance figures at a political debate, a ballet, a dramatic production, and a rock concert, all of which were held on the same night;
   e. number of calories you consume over a four-week period;
   f. number of people entering a museum each hour it is open;
   g. number of people entering each of four pizza places during one hour.

PROBLEMS

1. Find the median of each distribution below.

a.
X	f
8	3
7	6
6	7
5	6
4	1

b.
Class Interval	f
45–47	3
42–44	5
39–41	7
36–38	8
33–35	6
30–32	5
27–29	7
24–26	3
21–23	2
18–20	2

c.
Class Interval	f
30 and up	14
25–29	9
up to 24	6

d.
Class Interval	f
73–77	2
68–72	3
63–67	5
58–62	7
53–57	8
48–52	8
43–47	7
38–42	4
33–37	2
28–32	1

2. The general result of damage to the left cerebrum of a right-handed person is a lower IQ. (Presumably this is due to

18

reduced ability in logical, convergent thinking--a left-brain function.) Jeanette McGlone asked if this conclusion was true for both men and women. (This is a fairly typical example of extending knowledge--finding out if what is true for a population is also true for each sub-group.) The numbers below are IQ scores for left-brain damaged, right-handed females. The mean of these numbers is the same as that found by McGlone. Group these data into an appropriate frequency distribution, draw a graph, and find any measures of central value that are appropriate. Do these data constitute a population or a sample?

78	119	94	88	113	126	103	81
100	103	103	98	105	90	74	101
89	96	85	100	96	100	88	111
98	93	121	110	113	79	99	

3. A small group of people in a college town set out to promote greater use of bicycles. One member of the group was a statistician who was eager to measure progress as it was made. Shortly after the group agreed on its goal, she assessed five different modes of transportation by asking people how they got to work or school that morning. Responses were scored as auto--0, bicycle--1, motorcycle--2, walk--3, bus--4. Arrange the following scores into an appropriate frequency distribution and graph them. Calculate any measures of central value that are appropriate.

4	1	0	0	3	0	2	0	4	0
3	1	0	4	0	0	0	2	0	0
0	0	2	0	0	4	0	0	2	0
1	0	4	0	3	0	0	4	0	2

4. A psychology student stationed himself at a busy intersection. Each time he saw a man look at his watch, he would stop him and ask what time it was. A refusal to answer was scored as 0, giving the time without looking again at the watch as 1, and giving the time after looking at the watch a second time as 2. The following scores were obtained. Arrange them into an appropriate frequency distribution, and draw a graph. Calculate any measures of central value that are appropriate.

2	2	2	0	2	1	2
1	2	2	2	2	1	2
2	2	2	2	2	2	0

5. Arrange each set of scores into a grouped frequency distribution. The median of each distribution is given in the answer (for those of you who need additional practice in finding the median).

A.	50	40	55	57	59	42	44	44
	39	36	42	31	52	50	40	43
	39	35	61	57	49	57	60	67
	51	50	40	37	42	52	62	50

B.	29	39	49	27	37	47	52
	39	17	18	21	60	42	51
	12	19	29	42	61	4	8
	27	68	38	17	0	17	14
	0	3	47	48	29	21	17

CHAPTER 3   VARIABILITY

SUMMARY

Even if you have not studied the standard
deviation before, you have thought about,
expressed, and had expressed to you the idea of
variability in a population. In most expressions the idea was not presented quantitatively.
With the standard deviation, however, it is.
The standard deviation gives you a quantitative
measure of the variety in the population (or
sample).

Expressing an idea in a quantitative way
can be very powerful. You already have had a
good bit of experience with this; you have used
the mean as a quantitative expression of "the
typical member" for years now. Just think of
how often you resort to a mean when you want to
get across the concept of the typical member of
a group.

In a similar way, the standard deviation
tells you the average amount that scores differ
from the mean. After working with the standard
deviation, you will find it a powerful and
accurate way to express the concept of
variability.

In a very real way the three preceding
paragraphs are good examples of what will happen
during the rest of this course. A concept that
you understand more or less vaguely will be
introduced and then followed by quantitative
methods for expressing the concept.

The first quantitative measure of variability in this chapter is the range, a simple and
easily calculated statistic. It is simply the
numerical distance between the highest and
lowest scores.

In the sections on the standard deviation,
you are shown two ways to arrange the arithmetic
--the deviation-score method and the raw-score
method. The principal reason we presented you

with the deviation-score method was for teaching
purposes; it helps you understand what a standard deviation is and how the arithmetic works.
For most data analysis, though, we recommend the
raw-score formula. It is more accurate and
easier to use with a calculator.

Keeping the symbols s, S, and σ separated
and knowing which ones have N in the denomina-
tors and which one has N-1 takes a little
memorization. More difficult is recognizing
what situations call for s, S, or σ. Deciding
to use σ is usually not too hard--σ is used when
you realize you have the entire population of
scores. s is used when you have a sample but
are interested in the variability of the population. This is of frequent interest, and s is
seen most often of the three standard deviations. S is used when you have a small group of
scores that would ordinarily be thought of as a
sample but they are the only scores of interest.

N-1 is used in the denominator of s, the
statistic that estimates σ. We guarantee that
if you worked the exercise described in the
footnote in the section, "s as an estimate of
σ," you will understand the "why" of N-1 much
better.

Frankly, we were not too impressed with our
Figure 3.2. In Figure 3.2 vertical lines equal
to one standard deviation were added to the
points that represented the means. Although the
idea is an excellent one, we weren't happy
trying to illustrate it on a graph with just two
points. We have an example later in the text
(Problem 28 in Chapter 8) that will illustrate
more convincingly the case that adding a variability dimension to a graph of means facili-
tates understanding.

The variance gets three short paragraphs in
the text, which is not indicative of its importance in the overall field of statistics. You
will learn more about variance in Chapters 9 and
10. As a descriptive index of variability, however, the variance is not nearly as useful as
its square root, the standard deviation.

The final section of this chapter introduced to you the z score as it is used to

describe the relation of a raw score to its fellow scores. Here is another example of quantitatively expressing a notion that you are already somewhat familiar with--a notion that a score's meaning comes from its relationship to other scores.

MULTIPLE-CHOICE QUESTIONS

1. If you divide measures of variability into a "describe-data-at-hand" category and an "infer-about-a-population" category, the statistic that is not like the others--the one that doesn't belong--is

    (1) σ;
    (2) s;
    (3) S.

2. Two distributions that have the same mean must have the same

    (1) range;
    (2) standard deviation;
    (3) variance;
    (4) none of the above.

3. Which of the following is (are) not mathematically possible if only one distribution is being considered?

    (1) range = s;
    (2) range = $\overline{X}$;
    (3) range = μ;
    (4) all of the above.

4. You will get a negative number as a standard deviation

    (1) when all scores are negative;
    (2) when the mean of the scores is negative;
    (3) either (1) or (2) is sufficient;
    (4) under no circumstances--standard deviations are always positive numbers.

5. An experimenter was interested in the variability of SAT scores in the new freshman class at her university. She obtained the scores from the registrar. She should compute

    (1) $\bar{X}$;
    (2) s;
    (3) S;
    (4) z scores for each person.

6. Which of the following statements is <u>not</u> concerned with variability?

    (1) Sometimes we catch fish, and sometimes we don't.
    (2) Six-year-olds cannot thread a needle.
    (3) The team is inconsistent from week to week.
    (4) The range of scores is 85.

7. Which of the following is false?

    (1) $\Sigma x = 0$.
    (2) A raw score equal to the mean has a z score equal to 1.00.
    (3) z scores generally range from -3 to +3 for N = 100 or less.
    (4) Positive z scores represent raw scores above the mean.

8. The z score closest to zero represents a raw score

    (1) closest to the mean;
    (2) that is near the bottom of the distribution;
    (3) that is the lowest score in the distribution;
    (4) that is the highest score in the distribution.

9. For a set of scores, the sum of the deviation scores will be zero

   (1) when half the scores are negative;
   (2) when the mean is zero;
   (3) only when the standard deviation is zero;
   (4) always.

10. From all the employees in a company, a small group was selected to participate in a study of employee satisfaction. The results of the study were to be generalized to all the employees of the company. To find the variability in satisfaction, the investigator should compute

    (1) $\bar{X}$;
    (2) S;
    (3) s;
    (4) σ.

11. For a sample of 100 or fewer, the standard deviation could be about _____ the range. (Be careful on this one.)

    (1) 2 times;
    (2) 5 times;
    (3) 2-5 times;
    (4) one-fourth.

12. On the first test of material on dinosaurs, a class of sixth graders had a mean score of 36 with S = 12. The teacher was disappointed and assigned six pages of homework on dinosaurs and scheduled a second test. The top one-fourth of the class studied the extra material and did even better on the second test. The other three-fourths ignored the material and made the same score as before. Pick the mean and standard deviation that might be found, given the description.

    (1) $\bar{X}$ = 36, S = 12;
    (2) $\bar{X}$ = 36, S = 18;

(3) $\overline{X} = 42$, $S = 18$;
(4) $\overline{X} = 42$, $S = 12$.

13. Which of the following may be a negative number?

    (1) range;
    (2) variance;
    (3) deviation score;
    (4) both 2 and 3.

14. Which of the following statistics is also called a "standard score"?

    (1) s;
    (2) σ;
    (3) x;
    (4) z.

15. You can find the variance by performing one arithmetic operation on

    (1) the mean;
    (2) the standard deviation;
    (3) the range;
    (4) none of the above.

SHORT-ANSWER QUESTIONS

1. In this problem the question is, "How can I buy groceries cheaply and efficiently?" Suppose there are four equally convenient supermarkets and they all place advertisements in the newspaper on Wednesday. From these advertisements you have noted the prices for red delicious apples (per pound), 1/2 percent milk (per gallon), and Froot Loops cereal (per 12 oz). From your notes you have calculated the standard deviations of the prices. The results are: Apples--$.10, Milk--$.02, Cereal--$.01. Now suppose you are going out to buy the three items and you want to do it cheaply and efficiently. You have this week's ads. What do you do?

2. Tell what each of the three standard devia-
    tions is used for, that is, which are used
    on samples, and which are used on
    populations.

PROBLEMS

1. In the local punt, pass, and kick competi-
    tion, participants competed in three cate-
    gories: 8- and 9-year-olds, 10- and 11-
    year-olds, and 12- and 13-year olds.
    There were five participants in each age
    group. Below are their distance scores (in
    yards) for the pass. Relative to the par-
    ticipants' own groups, who was the overall
    winner?

8- to 9- Year-Olds		10- to 11- Year-Olds		12- to 13- Year-Olds	
Joe	28	Archie	32	Billy	51
Fran	25	Dan	30	Bob	49
Terry	22	Roger	26	George	45
Kenny	19	Jim	23	Sonny	42
Steve	16	Ken	20	John	38

2. A student in nursing read in her textbook
    that neonates (newborn babies) spend an
    average of 18 hours sleeping during their
    first day in the "outside world." She
    wondered how much variation there was from
    this average, so she observed the first day
    of life for 25 babies in the nursery of a
    large metropolitan hospital. She obtained
    the following data (hours spent sleeping).
    Decide whether to compute s, S, or σ and
    then compute it.

X	f
20	3
19	4

X	f
18	10
17	5
16	2
15	1

3. "What do you mean, you made a 60 on the inorganic final?" roared Dr. Phitt. "Why, when I was a pre-med student at dear old Beriberi University, I never made below an 80 in anything, and I expect you to uphold the family name there"! Below are two distributions of scores on an inorganic chemistry final--one distribution is for the class attended by young Ina and the other for her father's class 30 years earlier. Dr. Phitt had, as he said, scored 80 on the exam. Who, in fact, did better in the course?

Ina's Class	Dr. Phitt's Class
82	97
79	96
76	95
75	88
73	87
70	82
68	80
67	79
64	77
62	75
61	
60	
57	
52	
51	

4. The Clock Test is a technique for studying human vigilance--the ability to detect changes in stimulus events over relatively long periods of time. In the Clock Test, a hand moves regularly at one step per second, but sometimes, at random intervals, it will jump two steps. The subject's task is to notice the two-step jumps and press a button. Below are the percentages of stimuli missed by a group of 15 subjects during the first 15 minutes of a two-hour watch. Estimate σ and σ^2 using the raw-score method.

22	19	17	16	15	15	14	14
13	12	12	11	10	9	8	

5. In the Clock Test experiment described in Problem 4, the percentages of missed stimuli during the last 15 minutes of the two-hour watch are much higher. Estimate σ and σ^2, and write a sentence about the effect of two hours of vigilance on variability.

45	41	38	35	34	32	29	28
27	25	24	21	17	15	12	

6. Over a period of many years, Arnold Gesell and his associates studied the developmental rates of thousands of children. They were interested in, among other things, the average ages at which children could perform various motor skills, such as holding the head erect, rolling from back to stomach, and walking without support. Assume that the following data were collected on the age (in months) at which 200 babies first walked without support. What would you report to parents as the age at which they could expect their baby to exhibit this behavior? (Variability in age would be important information for the parents.)

Class Interval	f
24−26	5
21−23	9
18−20	43
15−17	53
12−14	48
9−11	34
6−8	8

CHAPTER 4 CORRELATION AND REGRESSION

SUMMARY

This is a chapter about correlation and regression, two different statistics that are closely related mathematically. They are used, however, for different purposes. A <u>correlation coefficient</u>, by itself, is used to describe the degree and the direction of a relationship between two variables. A <u>regression equation</u>, by itself, is used to draw a line of best fit and to predict scores on one variable, given scores on the other variable. Both of these statistical methods require a bivariate distribution, which is a distribution of two variables whose scores are logically paired. For the methods described in the text, the two variables must also have a linear relationship.

As in Chapter 3, you are presented with two methods of arranging your arithmetic when you calculate r. If you choose to use the "blanched" (partially cooked) formula, be sure to carry three or four decimal places in your calculations.

There are several different interpretations or stories that can be told by looking at a correlation coefficient. The algebraic sign gives the direction of the relationship, which is either direct (positive) or inverse (negative). The closer the absolute value of r comes to 1.00, the greater the strength of the relationship and the more confidence you can put in a prediction made from the regression equation. High correlation coefficients indicate reliable measurements. r^2 gives the <u>coefficient of determination</u>, the proportion of variance the two variables have in common. Correlation coefficients, no matter how large, are not sufficient to establish a causal relationship between the two variables. Finally, low correlations do not necessarily mean that there is no relationship

between the two variables: nonlinear relationships and truncated ranges both produce spuri-
ously low correlation coefficients.

Besides the Pearson product-moment correlation coefficient described in this chapter,
there are other kinds of correlation coefficients. What they have in common is that they
all express the strength of relationship between
variables.

Scientists are usually quite happy when
they can write the equation that gives the
relationship between two variables. If the
relationship is linear and if the correlation
coefficient is high, a regression equation is
often a quite satisfactory way to produce this
happiness.

MULTIPLE-CHOICE QUESTIONS

1. In order to use the regression equation
   technique described in your text, you must
   have

   (1) a logical pairing of the scores on the
       two variables;
   (2) a linear relationship between the two
       variables;
   (3) quantitative scores on both variables;
   (4) all of the above.

2. A Pearson correlation coefficient is appropriate to describe which of the situations
   below?

   (1) As X increases, Y decreases by the
       same amount.
   (2) As X increases, Y goes up at first
       slowly and then faster.
   (3) As X increases, Y goes up at first
       and then goes down.
   (4) All of the above.

3. Quantification is the idea that

    (1) all things can be counted;
    (2) all physical things can be counted;
    (3) the numerical representation of a
         phenomenon gives the most important
         picture;
    (4) a phenomenon can be better understood
         if its important parts are expressed
         as numbers.

4. A linear relationship is described by which
    of the statements below?

    (1) The two variables are paired in some
         logical fashion.
    (2) For every one-point increase in one
         variable, you get a four-point
         increase in the other variable.
    (3) Both of the above.
    (4) Neither of the above.

5. Suppose you had the exam scores on the
    first hour exam for 100 general psychology
    students. A correlation coefficient could
    be calculated if the scores were divided
    according to the variable _____.

    (1) gender--males and females;
    (2) where a person sits in the class--
         front or back;
    (3) both of the above;
    (4) neither of the above.

6. A Pearson product-moment correlation
    coefficient can be used to express the
    degree of relationship for which situa-
    tion(s) below?

    (1) A little anxiety produces poor
         results, a moderate amount produces
         good results, and a high level of
         anxiety produces poor results.
    (2) Early in training each trial helps
         only a little, but as training

33

progresses each trial causes a larger and larger gain.

(3) For every extra year of growth in a pine forest, you can expect an increase of 10,000 board feet.

(4) All of the above.

7. "For the last ten years, I've used smaller and smaller amounts of pesticide, and each year I've had fewer bugs and larger yields." The correlation between amounts of pesticide and number of bugs is

(1) positive;
(2) negative;
(3) zero;
(4) not determinable from the information given.

8. Identify the <u>incorrect</u> statement.

(1) A negative correlation is obtained when high scores on X go with low scores on Y and low scores on X go with high scores on Y.
(2) A positive correlation is obtained when high scores on X go with high scores on Y.
(3) A zero correlation is obtained when high scores on X go with both high and low scores on Y and low scores on X go with both high and low scores on Y.
(4) None of the above.

9. The coefficient of determination allows you to

(1) determine the variance two variables have in common;
(2) draw cause-and-effect statements;
(3) predict X scores, given Y scores;
(4) quickly determine the regression coefficients.

10. The least squares method of finding a formula for a straight line

    (1) produces a slope and an intercept;
    (2) makes the error in prediction a minimal amount;
    (3) was championed by Karl Pearson;
    (4) all of the above.

11. Pearson product-moment correlation coefficients can be used to establish the degree of relationship

    (1) even if the two variables are measuring different things;
    (2) even if the full ranges of the two variables are not included in the data;
    (3) even though the relationship is not linear;
    (4) all of the above.

12. The regression coefficient, a, is most clearly related to

    (1) the angle the regression line makes with the X axis;
    (2) the place the regression line crosses the Y axis;
    (3) the Y score predicted for an X score that is the mean of the X distribution;
    (4) the absolute size of the correlation coefficient.

13. Which of the following is (are) possible?

    (1) Two correlations of .30 and .70 that have the same b.
    (2) Two correlations of .30 and .70 that have the same a.
    (3) Both (1) and (2) are possible.
    (4) Neither (1) nor (2) is possible.

14. Suppose you know that the regression coefficients for the line that predicts the

height of pine trees from annual rainfall
are a = 10, b = -1.0.   Knowing this, you
can conclude that the correlation coefficient for these data is

(1)   positive;
(2)   negative;
(3)   perfect;
(4)   none of the above.

15.   Error in a regression analysis is defined
as

(1) Y';
(2) $Y - Y'$;
(3) $Y' - Y$;
(4) $(Y - Y')^2$.

SHORT-ANSWER QUESTIONS

1.   "The self-confidence of that group of
recruits is negatively correlated with
their success in the obstacle course."
Tell what this statement means.

2.   Describe the statistical method of regression.   Tell what it is good for and what
its limitations are.

3.   A problem in measuring personality is the
tendency of people to give a socially
desirable response to questions on personality tests rather than give a response
truly reflective of their own personali-
ties.   (Items like, "I am a hard worker"
and "I don't care what happens to my
neighbors" differ in their social desirability.)   In order to account for this
variable, it is important to measure
responses for their social desirability
(often on a scale of 1 to 9).   Studies have
been done using such widely diverse groups
as college students, schizophrenics, alco-
holics, sexual deviants, nuns, and geriat-
ric cases.   Suppose a group of nuns and a

group of sex offenders were both asked to
rate the social desirability of responses
to 50 personality test items on a scale of
1 to 9. Most such studies have found
results similar to those that follow.

$$r = .95$$
$$\bar{X} \text{ (nuns)} = 5.86$$
$$\bar{Y} \text{ (sex offenders)} = 5.59$$
$$S_x = 1.32$$
$$S_y = 1.46$$

a. Use words to explain the meaning of
this correlation coefficient.
b. Predict the rating given by sex offenders for a response rated 4.30 by the
nuns.

4. In a study of 4138 students in 25 law
schools, a correlation of .36 was found
between first-year law school grades and
scores on the Law School Admission Test.
Interpret the meaning of this correlation.

5. A small college was preparing data to present to an accreditation agency. Since the
standardized admissions test scores (ACT)
on entering freshmen were low, the college
decided to show that its students grew in
knowledge and academic skills while attend-
ing school. Juniors were therefore re-
tested with the ACT, and their scores were
paired with their scores as entering freshmen. The mean score improved from 15 to
21. The correlation coefficient was .60.
Write an interpretation.

PROBLEMS

1. Studies of conformity usually require that
some judgment be made by a subject concerning some stimulus. Group pressure is then
applied by everyone else agreeing to a

judgment that differs from the subject's judgment. The subject then judges the stimulus again and the amount of change is recorded as the dependent variable. A typical finding is embedded in the data below for you to discover. Here, each subject experiences conformity pressure in two situations. The first involves distance judgments--the judged distance between two widely spaced points. The second involves value judgments--the degree of agreement with ten controversial statements. What relationship is there in the two sets of change scores? Write an interpretation. (In addition to r and an interpretation, we have included the regression coefficients in our answer if you would like to calculate these statistics.)

Subject	Distance Judgments	Value Judgments
1	8	1
2	4	2
3	7	0
4	9	3
5	3	1
6	0	2
7	4	0

2. A nutritionist believed that the percent of children's body fat would be related to the percent of the "junk food" in their diets. He had the children keep a record of everything they ate over a two-week period and then computed the percent of the food classified as "junk." Later, he measured the children for percent of body fat. His data follow.

Subject	% Junk Food (X)	% Body Fat (Y)
1	46	40
2	32	43
3	29	28
4	23	31
5	20	36
6	17	25
7	15	20
8	12	12
9	11	15
10	8	19

a. Compute r.
b. Construct a scattergram and draw the regression line.
c. Predict the percent of body fat of a child whose diet is 25% junk food.
d. Describe the effect on body fat of eating junk food.

3. Many studies in psychology have been conducted to discover the nature of creativity. Some studies have examined the relationship between scores on verbal creative-thinking tests and on the ability to produce humor. A verbal creative-thinking test might measure the subjects' ability to make semantic transformations (thinking of different meanings for a word). A test of humor production might require subjects to make puns. Suppose the following scores were obtained from a group of ten subjects on these two measures. Analyze the data and write an explanation.

Subject	Semantic Transformation (X)	Puns (Y)
1	60	28
2	57	32

Subject	Transformation (X)	Puns (Y)
3	52	24
4	46	16
5	41	21
6	38	14
7	32	18
8	29	11
9	25	9
10	19	12

4. An elementary school teacher hypothesized that reading would improve vocabulary. To check this hypothesis, she recorded the number of minutes spent reading by some children in her sixth-grade class during their free period. She then gave them a 30-item vocabulary test. Analyze her data, interpret the results, and comment on her hypothesis.

Student	Time Spent Reading (X)	Vocabulary (Y)
1	45	21
2	42	26
3	35	24
4	31	18
5	26	20
6	22	19
7	17	15
8	12	17
9	10	12
10	8	16
11	5	11
12	1	6

CHAPTER 5   THEORETICAL DISTRIBUTIONS INCLUDING THE NORMAL DISTRIBUTION

SUMMARY

   This first chapter on inferential statistics presents two main ideas.

1.   The normal curve is a theoretical distribution that is widely used in statistics.

2.   You can use theoretical distributions to get information about the probability of actual events.

   Three kinds of theoretical distributions were described and illustrated--a rectangular distribution (with playing cards as an example), a binomial distribution (with coins as an example), and the normal distribution (with several examples). Each of these distributions was used for the same purpose--to find the probability of a particular event or set of events.
   The chapter illustrates the method of using a theoretical curve to make predictions about actual events, primarily with the normal curve. With the normal curve, the method involves these steps. Assume (or obtain evidence) that there is a correspondence between the empirical distribution of events you are interested in and the normal distribution. Using the mean and standard deviation of the empirical events and the particular events you are interested in, find the proportion of the theoretical curve that corresponds to the events of interest. (That is, find a z score and enter the normal curve table to find a proportion.) Finally, use that proportion as the probability of the future occurrence of the events you are interested in. This same probability can also be used to find

the expected number of events by multiplying the probability by the total number of events.

This same line of reasoning can be used in reverse, too. You can start with a proportion of the events and end up with the particular events that will encompass such a proportion.

Drawing pictures of theoretical distributions was recommended as a good way to conceptualize a problem. The ability to draw a curve and label the knowns and unknowns is evidence that you understand the problem. Once you understand it, working out the answer involves only a little algebra.

MULTIPLE-CHOICE QUESTIONS

1. The difference between an empirical distribution and a theoretical distribution is that a theoretical distribution

    (1)   is based on many more observations;
    (2)   is theory and cannot be used;
    (3)   is based on mathematics and logic;
    (4)   is based solely on observations.

2. Which of the following is an empirical distribution?

    (1)   the names and their frequencies of all high school graduates in the United States for the year 1900;
    (2)   the scores expected from an infinite number of throws of one die;
    (3)   the normal distribution in Table C in your text;
    (4)   all of the above.

3. In order to use the theoretical normal curve, which of the following things about the population must be known?

    (1)   mean;
    (2)   standard deviation;
    (3)   the form of the distribution;
    (4)   all of the above.

4. The term <u>normal distribution</u> was adopted because

    (1) the results were found only with normal, healthy individuals;
    (2) Sir Francis Normal was the first to write the equation for the curve;
    (3) results were first applied by teachers who had been trained in teachers' colleges, which, in those days, were called Normal Schools;
    (4) none of the above.

5. The area under the curve of a standard normal distribution is

    (1) dependent on the number of frequencies;
    (2) dependent on the size of the mean;
    (3) 1.00;
    (4) none of the above.

6. The theoretical normal curve has a mean equal to _____ and a standard deviation equal to _____ .

    (1) 1.00, 0.00;
    (2) 0.00, 1.00;
    (3) 1.00, 1.00;
    (4) 1.00, the standard deviation of the population.

7. If you were given one z score from a population of measurements and nothing else, you could determine

    (1) the mean of the population;
    (2) the standard deviation of the population;
    (3) both of the above;
    (4) neither of the above;

8. If an empirical distribution is converted to a distribution of z scores,

(1) the new mean will be zero;
(2) the new standard deviation will be 1;
(3) both of the above;
(4) neither of the above.

9. .4332 of the normal curve lies between μ and 1.5σ. The proportion between μ and $.75\sigma$ is

(1) .8664;
(2) .2166;
(3) .0668;
(4) not determinable from the information given.

10. Which of the following is a theoretical distribution?

(1) Twenty pennies were tossed in the air. When they landed, the number of heads was recorded. The 20 pennies were tossed 1000 times.
(2) The price of every house sold in the last five years in Grundy County was obtained from courthouse records.
(3) The number of persons who arrived late was recorded every time a general psychology class met during the semester.
(4) None of the above.

11. Bud and Lou were arguing about scores on the Ace Slap-Stick Comedy Test. These scores are distributed normally with a mean of 50. They agreed that 10% of the population had scores of 60 or better (and they were correct on this). Bud also claimed that 10% of the population had scores of 40 or below.

(1) Bud is correct.
(2) Bud is correct but only because each score point is worth one percentage point.

(3)   Bud is mistaken.
(4)   More information is necessary before a
      decision can be made.

12. Continuing the example of the Ace Slap-
     Stick Comedy Test, Bud claimed that,
     because 10% of the population had scores of
     60 or better, which is 10 points from the
     mean, 5% must have had scores of 70 or
     better, because doubling the score distance
     always halves the percentage.

     (1)   Bud is correct.
     (2)   Bud is mistaken.
     (3)   More information is necessary before a
           decision can be made.

13. Suppose the mean of a particular normal
     distribution is 3.95. The median of this
     distribution will be

     (1)   larger than 3.95;
     (2)   smaller than 3.95;
     (3)   3.95;
     (4)   not determinable from the information
           given.

14. Suppose that if k should occur, it will be
     called a success. If j should occur it
     will be called a failure. The ratio $\frac{k}{k+j}$ is

     (1)   the empirical probability of k;
     (2)   the empirical probability of j;
     (3)   the theoretical probability of k;
     (4)   the theoretical probability of j.

SHORT-ANSWER QUESTIONS

1. Distinguish between theoretical and
    empirical distributions.

2. Write a paragraph describing the normal
    curve.

3. Your text has some questions about hobbits, mythical creatures in J.R.R. Tolkien's books. Hobbits have furry feet and love to play games. Suppose some practical joker shaved the feet of the hobbits and reduced their height by one inch. What effect would this have on the mean and standard deviation? Drawing two pictures of the distribution of heights "before" and "after" will help you conceptualize this problem.

PROBLEMS

1. Identify each of the following distributions as theoretical or empirical.

    a. Twelve quarters were tossed in the air 500 times. Each time they landed, the number of heads was recorded.
    b. At Collegiate University the Registrar recorded the grade point average of every freshman for the years 1950, 1960, 1970, and 1980.
    c. For all Saturdays since the college began, the proportion of rainy days was determined from official weather records.
    d. Each offspring of a single fruit fly was classified as red-eyed or white-eyed.
    e. A normal-shaped distribution was found when 1000 needles from a white pine tree were measured.
    f. When pilots in the Japanese Air Force were weighed, the distribution was positively skewed.

2. Pygmies live in Zaire (formerly the Belgian Congo) in a region called Ituri (after the river by that name). Colin Turnbull, who lived with a group of pygmies during the early 1950s, wrote a delightful book called The Forest People (1961) telling of his experiences. Turnbull reports that pygmies

are less than 4 1/2 feet tall. For each of the questions below assume that the height of pygmies is normally distributed with a mean of $4'3''$ and a standard deviation of 2 inches.

a. Pygmies live in huts made up of a framework of branches covered with leaves. Materials can be gathered and the hut constructed in an afternoon. If the opening is 4 feet high, what proportion of the pygmies will have to duck to enter?

b. Pygmy culture has very few rules. We will make one up in order to have a question. Suppose only those pygmies who were between $4'2''$ and $4'6''$ tall were allowed to sing in a molino ceremony. What proportion would be left out?

c. In the group Turnbull lived with, there was a main group of about 20 families (65 people) plus a subsidiary group of about 4 families (15 people) led by Cephu. If one person from the camp were chosen at random, what is the probability that the person would be from Cephu's subgroup?

3. A classical experiment in extrasensory perception (ESP) consists of asking a subject to tell, without looking, the suit of each card in a deck of Zener cards. There are five suits in the deck so the probability of a chance match between the guess and the card is 1/5 or .20. If only chance is operating, you would expect a subject to get 20 matches if he made 100 guesses (.20 × 100 = 20). The standard deviation for this mean of 20 is 4.

a. What is the probability of a subject making 23 or more matches in 100 guesses?

b. What is the probability of 27 or more matches in 100 guesses?

c. Suppose a friend of a friend claimed to have ESP and agreed to sit just one time and guess at 100 cards. Suppose she made 36 matches. Calculate the probability of this many, or more, matches if only chance is at work, and carefully write a conclusion.

d. What is the probability of drawing a face card (jack, queen, or king) from a well-shuffled deck of cards?

4. R.B. D'Agnostino (1973) wrote a delightful article about the weight of a 40-pound box of bananas. The problem facing the banana shipper is the rule that a 40-pound box must weigh <u>at least</u> 40 pounds upon arrival. Suppose a shipper knows from past experience that, when boxes are packed to have 40 pounds, the standard deviation is four ounces and that on the average a box loses eight ounces in transit.

a. What mean weight should the shipper establish so that only one-fourth of 1% (.0025) of the boxes will arrive with less than 40 pounds?

b. Suppose the shipper adopts the weight you established and ships out 5 million boxes. How many will arrive with less than 40 pounds of bananas?

5. For the data in Figure 5.1, "Theoretical distribution of 52 draws from a deck of playing cards," the mean is 7.00 and the standard deviation is 3.74. (An ace gets a score of 1, jack = 11, queen = 12, king = 13.) Use the normal curve table to answer the following questions.

a. What proportion of the distribution would be expected to be 1's (aces)?

b. Compare this proportion to that given in Figure 5.1.

c. Tell why your calculated proportion is less than that given in Figure 5.1 in your text.

48

6. Royal Canadian Air Force (RCAF) pilots have a mean height of 177.4 cm (5'9.8") with a standard deviation of 6.1 cm. The mean height for U.S. Air Force pilots is 175.5 cm (5'9.1") (Van Cott and Kinkade, 1972). Assume that heights are normally distributed. Find the proportion of RCAF pilots who are taller than the mean of the U.S. pilots.

7. Women in the U.S. Air Force have hands that are 6.9 inches long on the average (from the tip of the middle finger to the heel of the hand). The standard deviation is .34 inches. Assume that hand length is normally distributed.

   a. What proportion have hands longer than 7 inches?
   b. What proportion would have hands shorter than 6 inches?
   c. What proportion would have hands 6.5 to 7.2 inches long?
   d. Of 3000 personnel, how many would have hands longer than 7.5 inches (the mean for male Air Force personnel)?
   e. How long would a woman's hand have to be to put her among the 10% with the longest hands?

CHAPTER 6 SAMPLES AND SAMPLING DISTRIBUTIONS

SUMMARY

The fundamental concept in Chapter 6 is the sampling distribution. A sampling distribution is a theoretical distribution of many (all possible) statistics, each of which was calculated from one of many (all possible) random samples drawn from a population. A sampling distribution is always for a particular statistic like the mean, variance, or correlation coefficient. The graph of a sampling distribution, then, is a picture of the effects that chance has when many random samples (each with its own statistic) are drawn from a population. The picture (and table) of these statistics can then be used when you need to determine the probability that a particular sample and its statistic came from a particular population.

Sampling distributions come in many shapes (as you will see in later chapters). However, the sampling distribution of the mean is a normal curve if the sample size is large enough.

There are few phrases or sentences in statistics that are worth memorizing; the Central Limit Theorem (CLT) is probably one of them. The CLT says that the form of the sampling distribution of the mean approaches a normal curve with a mean, μ, and a standard deviation, $\sigma/\sqrt{N}$, as N approaches ∞. This theorem is true regardless of the form of the population from which samples are drawn. The CLT applies only to the mean, but, fortunately, the mean is often the very statistic you are most interested in.

Because the sampling distribution of the mean is a normal curve, you can solve two kinds of statistical problems when you have large samples.

1. You can use the normal curve to find the probability that a particular sample mean came from a population with a known mean.

2. You can use the normal curve to establish an interval of scores within which you can expect (with a specified degree of confidence) the population mean to be.

Besides putting your faith in the CLT to produce a normal sampling distribution, you must also have faith that your sample is representative of the population you are interested in. To help justify these two instances of faith you should use large (over 30), random samples.

The mechanics of this chapter (z scores) are the same as those in Chapter 5. It's the concepts that are new and important in Chapter 6. One caution is in order about z scores. In Chapter 5 the z scores were based on scores known to be from the population. Thus, the z scores were generally from -3 to +3. In this chapter the z scores are based on means from a sample that may not be from the population. Thus, more extreme z scores may be found.

MULTIPLE-CHOICE QUESTIONS

1. According to your text, if you draw a random sample, you are assured that

   (1) the sample will always mirror the population;
   (2) you will be somewhat uncertain about the population;
   (3) the conclusions you draw will be correct;
   (4) none of the above.

2. The samples used by the Literary Digest to predict the outcome of presidential elections were

   (1) biased;
   (2) sometimes accurate;

(3)   both of the above;
(4)   neither of the above.

3.   The Central Limit Theorem (CLT) states that a sampling distribution of the mean approaches the normal curve if

(1)   the population is normally distributed;
(2)   the sample size is large;
(3)   the standard deviation is large;
(4)   any of the above is sufficient.

4.   A standard error is a measure of

(1)   central value;
(2)   variability;
(3)   correlation;
(4)   none of the above.

5.   Confidence intervals and hypothesis testing are parts of

(1)   descriptive statistics;
(2)   inferential statistics;
(3)   both (1) and (2);
(4)   experimental design.

6.   The word or phrase closest in meaning to the statistical meaning of the word error is

(1)   arithmetic mistake;
(2)   conceptual mistake;
(3)   deviation;
(4)   statistic.

7.   A 95 percent confidence interval of 14 to 17 means that

(1)   95 percent of the time μ will be between 14 and 17;
(2)   95 of the μ's will be between 14 and 17;

(3) 95 percent of the confidence intervals calculated like this one will contain μ;

(4) all of the above are correct.

8. When a stratified sample is used,

(1) only the best are polled;
(2) subcategories of the population are identified;
(3) the entire population is measured;
(4) the investigator is probably working in a brand-new area of research.

9. A biased sample is one that

(1) is too small;
(2) will always lead to a wrong conclusion;
(3) has certain groups from the population overrepresented or underrepresented;
(4) is always nonrepresentative.

10. The names of the mean and standard deviation of a sampling distribution are

(1) mean, standard deviation;
(2) mean, standard error;
(3) expected value, standard deviation;
(4) expected value, standard error.

11. As N becomes larger, $\sigma_{\bar{X}}$

(1) becomes smaller;
(2) becomes larger;
(3) gets closer in value to the mean;
(4) gets farther in value from the mean.

12. Uncertainty regarding conclusions about a population can be eliminated by

(1) drawing a sample;
(2) drawing a large sample;
(3) drawing a large, random sample;
(4) none of the above.

13. Prof. Gus LaPlace, the mad statistician, was fiddling around in his statistical laboratory one stormy winter night in 1801. He had a large pile of papers in front of him, each with a measurement written on it. "What would I get," he mused, "if I counted the number of papers I have, took the square root, and then divided that into the standard deviation of all the measurements? Hmmmmmm...Well, maybe I'll do it tomorrow," he said. If Prof. LaPlace had carried out his plan, he would have discovered (invented?)

   (1) the standard error of the standard deviation;
   (2) the standard error of the mean;
   (3) the standard error of the median;
   (4) none of the above.

14. When the participants in a study are assigned to a group on the basis of chance

   (1) random assignment has occurred;
   (2) random sampling has occurred;
   (3) the statistical conclusions will be exact;
   (4) all of the above.

15. Suppose you had a rectangular distribution (like that of the playing cards, pictured in Chapter 5). Suppose you drew many, many random samples of 25 scores and found the mean. If these means were arranged into a frequency distribution, you would expect the distribution to be

   (1) rectangular;
   (2) bimodal;
   (3) either of the above;
   (4) neither of the above.

SHORT-ANSWER QUESTIONS

1. Tell what the Central Limit Theorem (CLT) says.

2. a. Explain in words how you would obtain an empirical sampling distribution of the range (N = 50).
    b. Would the mean of this sampling distribution be close in value to the population range?

3. Distinguish between the concept of a sampling distribution and the sampling distribution of the mean.

PROBLEMS

1. Suppose you wanted to know whether the weight of vegetarians was less than that of the general population in the United States. Suppose also that you were fortunate enough to have the weights of a representative sample of 49 male vegetarians who were college age. Now, it is a fact that the average weight of 18- to 24-year-old male Americans (5' 10" tall) is 166 pounds (Statistical Abstract of the United States: 1987). It is also a fact that weight is not normally distributed but is positively skewed. Can you use the techniques described in Chapter 6 to determine the probability that the mean weight of college-age male vegetarians came from a population with a mean weight of 166? Write your conclusion and your reasoning.

2. Refer to Problem 1. Suppose you had the weights of the 49 vegetarians in kilograms. The sum of these weights was 3616 kg and the sum of squares of these weights was 271,456. What is the probability of obtaining such a mean weight (or one smaller) from a population with a mean weight of 75.4 kg (166 pounds)?

3. Here is a problem that uses statistical process control, the quality control method described in your text. For a particular component of a folding chair, a metal tube should be 74 inches long. Suppose a sample of 30 tubes, taken during a time when the manufacturing process was running well, produced the following statistics:

$$\Sigma X = 2217$$

$$\Sigma X^2 = 163,841.4$$

   a. Construct a 95 percent confidence interval about the sample mean. (Carry four decimal places in your calculations.)
   b. Suppose three weeks later a sample of 30 resulted in a $\Sigma X = 2223$. What conclusion is appropriate?

4. Draw a random sample with N = 6 from the following scores. Write down each step in your procedure.

   21 31 17 13 02 09 57 26 72 140

5. Most companies that manufacture light bulbs advertise their 100-watt bulbs as having a life of 750 hours. (Actually, this is an "it depends" statistic. In this case, it depends partly on the number of times the light is turned on and partly on whether or not the light is ventilated.) A consumer organization bought 50 bulbs and burned them until they failed. For the 50 bulbs, the mean number of hours was 725 and the standard deviation was 100. What is the probability of obtaining a mean this low or lower if the population mean for this brand of bulbs is 750 hours? Write a sentence about the advertised claims.

6. A teacher was interested in the mathematical ability of graduating high school seniors in her state. She gave a 32-item test to a random sample of 75 seniors with the following results: $\Sigma X = 1275$,

$\Sigma X^2 = 23,525$. Establish a 99% confidence interval about the sample mean, and write a sentence that explains the interval you found.

CHAPTER 7   DIFFERENCES BETWEEN MEANS

SUMMARY

This chapter is heavy with concepts of experimental design and the logic of inferential statistics. A simple experiment is described early in the chapter, one with two fairly large samples, each of which is treated differently. The two samples, which <u>might</u> be from different populations of scores, are measured on a dependent variable. The two sets of sample scores are analyzed statistically and, on the basis of the analysis, a conclusion is reached about the populations.

One possible conclusion is that the populations are different. This occurs when chance is an unlikely explanation for the difference between the two sample means. The other possible conclusion is that there is no strong evidence that the populations are different. This occurs when chance cannot be ruled out as an explanation for the difference between sample means.

The decision to attribute the observed difference to chance or to the experimental treatment is made by examining a sampling distribution of mean differences. This sampling distribution, which is a normal curve, is what happens when there is no <u>true</u> difference between the two populations (and, thus, all differences obtained between sample means are due to chance).

This sampling distribution, like all sampling distributions, shows the probability of various events if chance were responsible for the event. In this case the event is a difference between sample means.

If the "chance did it" explanation has a probability of .051 or greater, the obtained difference is attributed to chance. If the "chance did it" explanation has a probability of .050 or less, the obtained difference is attributed to the experimental treatment. The final step in the analysis of an experiment is a carefully worded conclusion about the effects of the experimental treatment on the dependent variable.

Several important terms are introduced in this chapter. The null hypothesis is the hypothesis that the two sets of scores come from two identical populations.

If your statistical analysis leads you to adopt the "chance did it" conclusion (and retain the null hypothesis) when, in truth, the populations are different, you have made a Type II error. Another way to make a mistake is to adopt the "experimental treatment caused the difference" conclusion (and reject the null hypothesis) when, in truth, the two sets of scores came from identical populations. This is a Type I error. The probability of a Type I error is symbolized α--a probability the experimenter can control. The probability of a Type II error is symbolized β; it is not directly under the experimenter's control.

The sampling distribution of mean differences shows all the possible outcomes of the experiment. Those outcomes that lead to rejection of the null hypothesis are said to fall in the critical region. The amount of the distribution in the critical region determines the level of significance (typically, the amount is .05 of the distribution). The critical region may be divided and placed in both tails of the sampling distribution (a two-tailed test) or it may all be assigned to one tail (a one-tailed test).

The factors that determine whether you will reject the null hypothesis in an experiment were explained in the text. They are:

1. the actual difference between the populations,

2. the size of the standard error of a difference, which is governed by sample size and sample variability, and

3. alpha.

MULTIPLE-CHOICE QUESTIONS

1. The sampling distribution of differences between means used in Chapter 7

   (1) has a mean of zero;
   (2) has a positive mean;
   (3) has a negative mean;
   (4) has a mean that depends on whether or not the two sets of sample scores come from the same population.

2. Which of the following is an example of an alternative hypothesis?

   (1) $\mu_1 = \mu_2$;
   (2) $\mu_1 - \mu_2 = 0$;
   (3) both of the above;
   (4) neither of the above.

3. A "significant" event in statistics is one that is

   (1) important;
   (2) true;
   (3) not attributed to chance;
   (4) all of the above.

4. Events that fall into the critical region are considered to be

   (1) due to chance;
   (2) not due to chance;
   (3) errors;
   (4) unfortunate, because the experiment will have to be run again.

5. Here is a good question that requires careful thinking. The logic of inferential statistics involves assuming

(1)　that two populations have equal means and then using sample data to conclude that they are probably equal;

(2)　that two populations have unequal means and then using sample data to conclude that they are probably unequal;

(3)　that two populations have equal means and then using sample data to conclude that they are probably unequal;

(4)　that two populations have unequal means and then using sample data to conclude that they are probably equal.

6.　Which answer below belongs with the concept of a two-tailed test of significance?

(1)　H_1:　$\mu_1 > \mu_2$;
(2)　Type II error;
(3)　both (1) and (2);
(4)　a divided critical region.

7.　Which of the following variables affects the size of the standard error of a difference?

(1)　difference between sample means;
(2)　sample size;
(3)　both of the above;
(4)　neither of the above.

8.　With respect to the null hypothesis, inferential statistics allows you to conclude

(1)　that it is probably true;
(2)　that it is probably false;
(3)　both (1) and (2) are possible using inferential statistics;
(4)　neither (1) nor (2) is possible using inferential statistics.

9.　Suppose samples were drawn from two populations that had different means. On the basis of the difference between the two sample means, the experimenter accepted H_1. Which answer describes this situation?

(1) Type I error;
(2) Type II error;
(3) correct decision;
(4) either (1) or (2) depending on whether a one- or two-tailed test was used.

10. A one-tailed test is proper when

(1) you do not have enough data for a two-tailed test;
(2) you have only one sample, not two;
(3) you are only interested in finding out if the effect of a treatment is to increase the scores;
(4) you want to make the standard error of a difference as small as possible.

11. The area of a sampling distribution that corresponds to unlikely events is called

(1) the significant area;
(2) the alpha level;
(3) the null hypothesis;
(4) the critical region.

12. Which conclusion is not appropriate when using inferential statistics?

(1) The two sample means probably came from two different populations.
(2) The two samples probably came from the same population.
(3) Retain the hypothesis that the two sample means came from the same population.
(4) All of the above.

13. With the aid of inferential statistics you can find the probability that the null hypothesis is

(1) false;
(2) true;
(3) both (1) and (2);
(4) neither (1) nor (2).

14. Suppose there were two identical popula-
    tions. An experimenter drew a random sam-
    ple from each and, on the basis of the
    sample data, concluded that the null
    hypothesis was false. Which of the follow-
    ing describes this situation?

    (1) Type I error;
    (2) Type II error;
    (3) correct decision;
    (4) (1) or (2) depending on the size of
         the sample.

15. According to your text the reason that
    experimenters conduct experiments is to

    (1) obtain a large z score;
    (2) find the truth about the two samples;
    (3) draw a conclusion about the
         populations;
    (4) all of the above.

16. The custom of using an α level of .05 got
    its start in the field of

    (1) astronomy;
    (2) agriculture;
    (3) physics;
    (4) government.

SHORT-ANSWER QUESTIONS

1. List the factors that influence whether or
   not you reject the null hypothesis.
   Explain how each factor influences the
   final decision.

2. A typical two-group experiment might have
   the phrase "p = .01." Explain this by
   finishing the sentence: The probability is
   .01 that ...

3. An undergraduate student in philosophy of
   science became intrigued with the notion of
   experimenter bias. Developed and

researched by Robert Rosenthal, the basic phenomenon is that experimenters bias their results according to their expectations. This undergraduate decided to repeat one of Rosenthal's studies. She sent students out to obtain data on "attitudes toward abortion," using a scale of -20 to +20. Half the students were led to believe that attitudes would be "generally favorable" and half that attitudes would be "generally unfavorable." Each of the 70 students obtained data from one person. The mean rating from those whose expectations were favorable was 10.3; for those whose expectations were unfavorable, the mean was 7.8. Using the techniques of Chapter 7, she found a z score of 1.05. What conclusion should be drawn?

4. In their book Alcohol and Old Age, Mishara and Kastenbaum (1980) reported the effects of the consumption of three to six ounces of wine per day on the well-being of elderly people. Results such as the following typify their findings. Suppose 80 randomly selected residents of a nursing home are randomly divided into two groups. One group is given a glass of wine with dinner each evening for a month, and the other group is not. All subjects are then given a test of self-confidence in which higher scores mean greater self-confidence. The mean for the wine-with-dinner group is 77.3, and that for the no-wine group is 72.9. The z score for this difference is 3.19. Write a statement of interpretation.

PROBLEMS

1. The problem that follows is one that you have probably seen before. It is the last problem in the chapter of the text. We really do think that your education in statistics will be improved if you will tackle

this problem. If you have already done it, accept our congratulations.

Write an essay on inferential statistics. We suggest that your essay not contain any reference to the normal curve because, as you will see, you can do inferential statistics without using the normal curve. A good procedure is to write down from memory the things you'd like to include. Then, go back over these last three chapters and make more notes of facts, considerations, or organizational ideas. Write the essay and revise it. Rest. Revise again and write a final answer.

2. This is an experiment on set (previous experience) that is from the same tradition as the "two-string problem" in your text. This experiment is based on one by Luchins (1942) and is referred to as the "water-jar problem." Subjects were told to (mentally) use three jars to measure out a specific amount of water. For example, if the jars held 12, 4, and 3 units and the task was to obtain 5 units, you could fill the 12-unit jar and from it fill the 4- and 3-unit jars once, leaving 5 units in the larger jar. After giving the kind of explanation you have just received, Luchins gave subjects the series of eight problems below. You will find it worthwhile to work these problems yourself, in order, noting in the margin the number of seconds it takes you to solve each problem. Work the eight problems before reading on.

Problem	Jars Contain			Obtain
1	21	127	3	100
2	14	163	25	99
3	18	43	10	5
4	9	42	6	21
5	20	59	4	31
6	23	49	3	20
7	15	39	3	18
8	28	76	3	25

Some subjects worked the problems in the order that you followed, and some started with Problem No. 8. The dependent variable was the amount of time necessary to solve Problem No. 8. The independent variable was whether the subject had received the "set" generated by Problems 1 through 7. (If you worked the problems as suggested, you established such a set.) The following data are in seconds. Analyze the data and write a conclusion.

	No Set--(Problem No. 8 first)	Set--(Problem No. 8 last)
ΣX	196	784
ΣX^2	976	14,272
N	49	49

3. For some things that you learn, the longer the time between learning and recall, the poorer the recall (forgetting). For some tasks, however, forgetting may not occur. The following data were obtained from subjects in a pursuit rotor study (Koonce, Chambliss, and Irion, 1964). The pursuit rotor is an eye-hand coordination task in which the subject is to keep a stylus on a small rotating disk. In the experiment all subjects practiced for five minutes. Half continued for two minutes, and the other

half "rested" for six months before doing the final two minutes. Time on target for these final two minutes was the dependent variable. Analyze the scores and write a conclusion.

Amount of Rest

	0	6 mos.
ΣX	51.2	76.8
ΣX^2	89.25	147.00
N	64	64

4. Analyze the data below with a two-tailed z score test.

	Group 1	Group 2
$\overline{X}$	0.8	1.2
s	2	2
N	64	64

5. Those interested in the nature of <u>Homo sapiens</u> have often cast questions in the form of "Is experience necessary for this behavior, or will it develop without any experience?" One way of answering this question has been to study different cultures. The rationale is that, if the cultures are quite different but the behavior is the same, then experience is not necessary. In the case of walking, a behavior of fundamental importance, comparisons have been made between American Indian cultures and Anglo American cultures. Some Indian babies spent most of the day bound to a board on their mothers' backs and had few opportunities to creep, crawl, and kick. The age (in months) at which children from the two cultures first walked was the dependent variable in this study. Analyze the data and write a conclusion.

	American Indian	Anglo American
ΣX	2,145	2,160
ΣX^2	33,238	33,687
N	144	144

CHAPTER 8   THE t DISTRIBUTION AND THE t TEST

SUMMARY

There are two new and important concepts in Chapter 8.   The t distribution is new to you and so is the distinction between independent-samples and correlated-samples designs.

The other important concepts in this chapter you have studied before.   You studied the notion of using a sampling distribution to find probabilities back in Chapter 6, and the t distribution is just another kind of sampling distribution.   The idea that an experiment can be designed so that the difference between two sample means can be attributed to chance or to the experimental treatment is familiar to you from your study of the logic of inferential statistics in Chapter 7.   The basic idea of a confidence interval was covered near the end of Chapter 6.

As mentioned in the text, the distinction between independent-samples designs and correlated-samples designs will appear again.   Correlated-samples designs occur when you have some logical reason for pairing scores from the two groups.   Natural pairs, matched pairs, and repeated measures are names for three of the situations in which scores are paired.   If there is no logical reason for pairing the scores, the design is an independent-samples one.

Chapter 8 contains a way to use a sampling distribution that you have not seen before.   The t distribution is used to determine the probability that a Pearson correlation coefficient obtained from a sample came from a bivariate population whose correlation is .00.

In summary, the t distribution in Chapter 8 was used to:

1. determine the probability of obtaining

    a. a particular sample mean from a popu-
       lation with a mean, μ;
    b. a particular difference between two
       independent-samples means if the sam-
       ples came from two identical
       populations;
    c. a particular difference between the
       means of two correlated samples if the
       samples came from two identical
       populations;
    d. a particular correlation coefficient
       from a bivariate population with a
       zero correlation;

2. establish a confidence interval about a
   difference between independent-samples
   means and correlated-samples means.

   Use of the t distribution is justified when
three conditions regarding the dependent variable scores are met. The three conditions are

1. they are normally distributed,

2. their variances are equal, and

3. they are random samples of the
   populations.

MULTIPLE-CHOICE QUESTIONS

1. A before-and-after design is an example of
   a _____ design.

    (1) repeated-measures;
    (2) natural-pairs;
    (3) matched-pairs;
    (4) all of the above.

2. In an independent-samples design, the null hypothesis is that

   (1) the population mean of one group is equal to that of a second group;
   (2) the population mean of one group is larger or smaller than that of a second group;
   (3) the sample mean of one group is equal to that of a second group;
   (4) the sample mean of one group is larger or smaller than that of a second group.

3. An experimenter found one sample mean of 13 based on an N of 8. The second sample mean was 18 based on an N of 6. The design

   (1) was a correlated-samples one;
   (2) was an independent-samples one;
   (3) could be either a correlated- or an independent-samples one.

4. If a 99% confidence interval about a difference between means is 2.31 to 24.62, the null hypothesis may be

   (1) rejected at the .01 level;
   (2) rejected at the .05 level;
   (3) both (1) and (2);
   (4) retained.

5. Which of the following is not an assumption necessary to justify using the t distribution to find probabilities?

   (1) The samples must be random samples from the populations.
   (2) The populations must have equal variances.
   (3) The populations must be normally distributed.
   (4) The populations must have equal means.

6. "_____ depends on the number of observations minus the number of relations among the observations" is a statement about how to calculate

(1) df;
(2) the difference between means;
(3) $s_{\bar{x}}$;
(4) none of the above.

7. In an independent samples design the Hatfields had a mean score of 25; the mean score of the McCoys was 26. Low scores mean better performance. The researcher ran a two-tailed test with α at .05. A t value of 1.99 was found.

(1) If df = 40, the Hatfields are significantly better than the McCoys;
(2) If df = 40, the McCoys are significantly better than the Hatfields;
(3) If df = 120, the Hatfields and the McCoys are not significantly different;
(4) If df = 120, the Hatfields are significantly better than the McCoys;
(5) If df = 120, the McCoys are significantly better than the Hatfields.

8. Which of the following statements is most closely related to confidence intervals?

(1) The sample correlation coefficient is significantly different from .00.
(2) The difference between the two population means is between .95 and .99.
(3) The difference between the two population means is not zero.
(4) The mean of the first population is greater than the mean of the second.

9. When the t distribution is used to determine the significance of a correlation coefficient, the null hypothesis is that the population correlation coefficient is

(1)   -1.00;
(2)   0.00;
(3)   1.00;
(4)   the coefficient obtained from the
      sample.

10.   A standard error of the difference, calcu-
      lated by the direct-difference method, was
      found to be 18.00.   The design of the
      experiment

      (1)   was a correlated-samples design;
      (2)   was an independent-samples design;
      (3)   could have been either a correlated-
            or an independent-samples design.

11.   The person who developed the t distribution
      was

      (1)   Adolphe Quételet;
      (2)   Francis Galton;
      (3)   Alex Guinness;
      (4)   W.S. Gosset.

12.   In an independent-samples design, the Dogs
      mean was 54.0 and the Cats mean was 53.9.
      Larger scores are better.   A t value of
      2.50 was calculated.   For a two-tailed test
      with α = .05, which conclusion is
      appropriate?

      (1)   If df = 5, Dogs are significantly
            better than Cats;
      (2)   If df = 4, Cats are significantly
            better than Dogs;
      (3)   If df = 8, Dogs are significantly
            better than Cats;
      (4)   If df = 8, Cats are significantly
            better than Dogs;
      (5)   If df = 9, Dogs are not significantly
            different from Cats.

13. Under which of the following conditions is the t distribution a normal curve?

   (1) When df = 1;
   (2) When the populations from which the samples are drawn are normal;
   (3) Both of the above;
   (4) Neither of the above.

14. A correlation of .45 based on 18 pairs of scores is

   (1) significant at the .05 level;
   (2) significant at the .01 level;
   (3) significant at the .001 level;
   (4) not significant.

15. A one-tailed test of significance produced a $t = -2.30$, significant at the .05 level. The design of this experiment

   (1) was a correlated-samples design;
   (2) was an independent-samples design;
   (3) could have been either a correlated- or an independent-samples design.

SHORT-ANSWER QUESTIONS

1. Describe the difference between a correlated-samples design and an independent-samples design.

2. Name the design of each of the following experiments and give the appropriate degrees of freedom.

   a. To determine which is the lowest form of humor, 14 sophomores rated a pun and then a limerick for lowness.
   b. To determine which is the lowest humor, a Greek physician found the amount of blood and the amount of lymph in the sole of each of 21 Greek philosophers.
   c. To determine which is the longest form of humerus, an anthropologist measured

that bone in 15 men and 15 women and compared the sexes.

d. To determine whether the psychologist or the philosopher had the lowest form of humus in his garden, 12 samples were taken from the garden of each. The amount of humus was determined for each sample.

e. Every student knows, of course, that the very lowest form of humor is test humor. To determine if test humor has become even lower over time, the tests of 34 young professors were compared for lowdownness to the tests of each of their own teachers when they were young.

3. Suppose a small college found a correlation of .40 between their standardized entrance examination (SAT) and first-semester freshman grades for 175 freshmen. Test the significance of this correlation coefficient, and write a sentence of explanation.

PROBLEMS

1. In an early study of the effects of frustration on feelings of hostility, Miller and Bugelski (1948) had a group of boys at a camp rate their attitudes toward two minority groups (Mexicans and Japanese). They then put the campers through a long and difficult testing session that kept them away from their weekly movie. Finally they had the boys rate their attitudes toward the minority groups again. The data below are similar to those obtained by Miller and Bugelski. Analyze the data, and explain what they found. (Scores represent the number of unfavorable traits attributed to minorities.)

Subject	Before Testing	After Testing
1	5	6
2	4	4
3	3	5
4	3	4
5	2	4
6	2	3
7	1	3
8	0	2

2. R.S. Lazarus (1964) had two groups of subjects watch a film that showed accidents occurring in a workshop. The accidents were gruesome events such as fingers being cut off and a plank being thrown through a man's midsection by a circular saw. One group of subjects was instructed to remain detached from the events. The other group was instructed to become involved. Increases in heart rate were recorded for all subjects. The data given below are similar to those obtained by Lazarus. Analyze the data and comment on human ability to control emotions (as measured by heart rate increase).

Detached	Involved
23	31
21	27
19	24
15	23
14	21
12	14
10	

3. A number of studies have used animals to examine possible relationships between neuroticism and alcoholism. Here is a

typical study of this type. Two cats were
randomly selected from each of seven lit-
ters. One cat from each litter was offered
milk spiked with 5% alcohol. Consumption
was measured. Their litter mates were
first subjected to a procedure designed to
induce experimental neurosis and then
offered the spiked milk. The amount consumed in three minutes was measured in
cubic centimeters for both groups. Establish a 95% confidence interval around the
difference between means of the data below,
and comment on the relationship between
neuroticism and alcohol consumption.

Litter- mates	No Experimen- tal Neurosis	Experimen- tal Neurosis
1	63	88
2	59	90
3	52	74
4	51	78
5	46	78
6	44	61
7	38	54

4. As a result of some of his research before
the turn of the century, E.L. Thorndike
concluded that animals were incapable of
learning by imitation. In 1901, however,
L.L. Hobhouse reported the results of
experiments with cats, dogs, otters, ele-
phants, monkeys, and chimpanzees indicating that they could learn by imitation.
Suppose the following study was carried
out. One group of hungry cats is shown
food being obtained from under a vase.
Another group is not. Shortly afterward,
time (in seconds) required to upset the
vase and find the food is recorded for
each animal. Results are given below.

Do these results support either of the two
theorists?

Shown	Not Shown
18	25
15	22
15	21
12	19
11	16
9	15

5. An industrial psychologist developed a new test to screen applicants for jobs on the company's assembly line. To see if the test was working (a validity test), she administered it to 20 consecutive applicants and hired them, no matter what their score. Foremen were instructed to keep them on the job for six weeks regardless of their performance. She then asked their foremen to rate each of them as a success or failure. (Two of the new employees had quit by then.) Below are their scores on the screening test. Establish a 99% confidence interval around the mean difference, and comment on how well the test works.

Foreman Rating

Success	Failure
31	19
28	17
27	16
24	13
23	12
22	10
21	9
19	7
18	
15	

6. The museum of natural science was having a
   snake show, and Dr. Loveless, the personality theorist, took advantage of the occa-
   sion to test his hypothesis that massive
   exposure to anxiety-arousing stimuli would
   reduce subsequent anxiety (a technique
   called flooding). From a large group of
   people, he measured anxiety toward snakes
   with a questionnaire and then used the
   scores to put together 12 matched pairs.
   He personally accompanied one member of
   each pair to the herpetological extravagan-
   za and saw to it that he or she viewed
   every exhibit. He then had all 24 fill out
   the questionnaire again. Analyze his data
   and use the results to evaluate his
   hypothesis.
   (High scores mean high anxiety.)

Pair Number	Did Not View Exhibits	Viewed Exhibits
1	44	45
2	40	36
3	39	37
4	36	33
5	35	32
6	34	36
7	32	32
8	28	29
9	23	19
10	23	18
11	19	19
12	15	14

CHAPTER 9   ANALYSIS OF VARIANCE: ONE-WAY CLASSIFICATION

SUMMARY

The most important thing for you to understand from this chapter is the rationale of
ANOVA.   To really understand ANOVA you must have
a clear idea of how the two estimates of the
population variance are found.   We have told
this story two different ways below, once in
list form and a second time with paragraphs and
pictures.

RATIONALE OF ANOVA--I

A.   Assume that the variances of the populations from which the samples were taken are
equal.
     Estimate this variance by calculating from
each sample a variance and averaging them.   Put
this variance aside for the time being.

B.   Recognize that when the null hypothesis is
true the sample means will be similar to each
other.   This variability can be measured with a
variance.
     Calculate this variance and multiply it by
a factor that will make it equal to the population variance that was estimated previously.
     Make a ratio with the second variance (the
one that measures the variability among sample
means) in the numerator and the first variance
(the one that measures the population variance)
in the denominator.
     Expect that this ratio will be about 1.00,
with variation expected because of sampling
variation.
     The sampling variation of this ratio has
been described using a sampling distribution;
ratio values that are less probable than .05 and
.01 have been tabled.

C.   Recognize that when the null hypothesis is
false the sample means will be different from
one another. This variability can be measured
with a variance, producing a value that will be
larger than that which occurs when the samples
come from the same population.

Calculate this variance and multiply it by
the factor used in the B part of this rationale.

Make a ratio with this variance (produced
by sample means drawn from different populations) in the numerator and the first variance
(the one that measures population variance) in
the denominator.

Expect that this ratio will be larger than
1.00.

D.   If the ratio produced by the data is larger
than the tabled value that has a probability of
only .05, conclude that the null hypothesis is
false.

RATIONALE OF ANOVA--II

Suppose you drew three random samples with
$N_1 = N_2 = N_3$ from the same population (H_0 is
true) and calculated the mean of each sample $\bar{X}_1$,
$\bar{X}_2$, and $\bar{X}_3$. These three sample means would
vary. You could measure the amount of this
variation by calculating the variance of the
three means. What will determine whether this
variance is large or small?

The expected size of the variance would
depend on the variability of the original population. In Figure 9.1, you can easily see that
the variance of three means drawn from population A would be much smaller than the variance
of three means drawn from population B. Thus, a
variance based on $\bar{X}_1$, $\bar{X}_2$, and $\bar{X}_3$ would depend on
the amount of variability in the population.

Fortunately, you can estimate the population variance. In fact, you can get three estimates, one from each sample. Each s^2 is an
estimate of σ^2. Those three estimates can then
be pooled to get a more reliable estimate of σ^2.

So, you now have two variances, one that is
calculated from the sample means and one that is

81

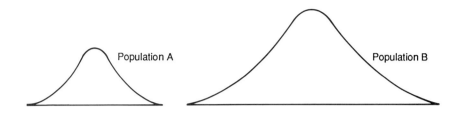

Figure 9.1 Two populations with different variability. The variability among sample means from Population A would be smaller than that among sample means from Population B.

an estimate of the population variance. It turns out that, when the variance calculated from the sample means is multiplied by the sample size, it becomes an estimate of the population variance. (See steps 1, 2, and 3 on p. 190 in the text.) Thus, when the null hypothesis is true, the ratio of the two variances, except for sampling fluctuations, will be approximately 1.00.

Now look at what happens when the null hypothesis is false. In this case the samples are not all drawn from the same population, so one or more of the sample means would be expected to be different from the others. Thus, the variance based on sample means will be larger when the null hypothesis is false. However, the estimate of the population variance based on the pooled sample variances will not be affected by the one or more deviant populations since the assumption is made that the population variances are equal. Thus, when the null hypothesis is false, you would expect the F value to be greater than 1.00.

The F distribution (Table F in your text) shows F values that would occur 5% and 1% of the time when the null hypothesis is true. If your experiment produces an F value that is larger than the tabled F value, you should reject the null hypothesis and conclude that the samples did not all come from the same population.

If the data allow you to reject the null hypothesis, further tests are required before you can say that one particular mean is significantly different from another. These tests fall into two categories, a priori and post hoc. A priori tests require that a limited number of comparisons be chosen on logical grounds before the data are examined. Post hoc tests allow you to make statistical comparisons after examining the data. One post hoc test, Tukey's Honestly Significant Difference, was described. Tukey's HSD allows you to make all pair-wise comparisons.

After conducting an ANOVA and applying any subsequent tests that are appropriate, your final task is to explain the results of the experiment using the terms of the independent and dependent variables.

The ANOVA technique described in your text is appropriate for analyzing quantitative data from independent samples if certain assumptions about the sampled populations are true. These assumptions are that the population variances are equal and that the populations are normally distributed. In addition, the technique assumes that the samples are drawn randomly from the populations.

MULTIPLE-CHOICE QUESTIONS

1. The person who developed ANOVA was

    (1) W.S. Gosset, a businessman;
    (2) George W. Snedecor, a psychologist;
    (3) "student," a pseudonym;
    (4) Ronald A. Fisher, a biologist.

2. An F distribution is a

    (1) normal distribution;
    (2) t distribution;
    (3) sampling distribution;
    (4) none of the above.

3. The null hypothesis tested by ANOVA is that

    (1) all samples have the same mean;
    (2) each sample is drawn from a different population;
    (3) the populations from which the samples are drawn have the same mean;
    (4) one or more of the populations from which the samples are drawn has a mean that is different from the others.

4. The ANOVA technique described in the text can be used on

    (1) correlated-samples designs;
    (2) independent-samples designs;
    (3) both (1) and (2);
    (4) neither (1) nor (2).

5. If the null hypothesis is true, _____ will be a good estimate of the population variance.

    (1) mean square within groups;
    (2) mean square between groups;
    (3) both of the above;
    (4) neither of the above.

6. Which symbol below will most quickly tell you the number of levels of the independent variable?

    (1) N;
    (2) K;
    (3) F;
    (4) SS.

7. The larger the population variance, the larger _____ is (are).

    (1) F;
    (2) df_{bg};
    (3) MS_{wg};
    (4) all of the above.

8. If the F value obtained from the data is larger than the tabled F value, you should

   (1) reject the null hypothesis;
   (2) retain the null hypothesis;
   (3) rework the problem, because such an answer is impossible.

9. Suppose MS_{bg} is calculated for three samples that are drawn from a population with a mean μ. Under which condition below would MS_{bg} certainly become larger?

   (1) the addition of a sample from a population with the same mean μ;
   (2) the addition of a sample from a population with a mean $\mu + \mu$;
   (3) both (1) and (2);
   (4) the removal of one of the three samples from the calculations.

10. Tukey's Honestly Significant Difference test is appropriate

    (1) when an ANOVA produces a significant $\underline{F}$;
    (2) when an ANOVA produces an insignificant $\underline{F}$;
    (3) in both cases above;
    (4) in neither case above.

11. Which of the following is not an assumption of analysis of variance?

    (1) All samples are drawn from the same population.
    (2) All samples are drawn from populations that have equal variances.
    (3) All samples are obtained by random sampling from the populations.
    (4) All samples are drawn from populations that are normally distributed.

12. A group of 72 subjects was equally divided into four groups. A Tukey's HSD produced a value that led to the conclusion that Mean

1 was significantly larger than Mean 2, $p <$ .05. Which of the following situations would lead to such a conclusion?

(1) $\bar{X}_1 = 7$, $\bar{X}_2 = 0$, $MS_{wg} = 80$;
(2) $\bar{X}_1 = 24$, $\bar{X}_2 = 13$, $MS_{wg} = 180$;
(3) both of the above;
(4) neither of the above.

13. A priori and post hoc are terms that refer to

(1) whether the null hypothesis should be rejected;
(2) whether the assumptions of ANOVA have been met;
(3) kinds of tests used after an ANOVA;
(4) all of the above.

14. Tukey's Honestly Significant Difference test is a _____ test.

(1) a priori;
(2) post hoc;
(3) both of the above;
(4) neither of the above.

15. A group of 36 subjects was equally divided into three groups. A Tukey's HSD produced a value that led to the conclusion that Mean 1 was significantly larger than Mean 2, $p <$ .05. Which of the following situations would lead to such a conclusion?

(1) $\bar{X}_1 = 9$, $\bar{X}_2 = 2$, $MS_{wg} = 50$;
(2) $\bar{X}_1 = 24$, $\bar{X}_2 = 14$, $MS_{wg} = 84$;
(3) both of the above;
(4) neither of the above.

INTERPRETATION

1. Florence Nightingale (1820-1910) was instrumental in reforming medical care. Her methods were based on her experience administering hospitals for British soldiers who

86

were casualties when England was fighting in Crimea (a peninsula in the Black Sea that now belongs to Russia). Part of Nightingale's success can be attributed to her pioneering use of statistics and graphs. She was especially appreciative of the earlier work of Quételet. (See Cohen in the March, 1984 issue of <u>Scientific American</u>.)

The "improvement scores" below will produce conclusions like those that Nightingale found when she compared patients in her military hospital in Crimea with civilian patients in English and French hospitals. Examine the summary data, calculate F and HSD values, and write your conclusions.

Hospital Located in

	Crimea	England	France
Means	15	9	8
N	12	12	12

Source	df	MS
Between Hospitals	2	124.52
Within Groups	33	20.62

2. Aronson and Mills (1959) studied three groups who were initiated into a sorority. One group experienced extreme embarrassment; a second, mild embarrassment; a third, no embarrassment. Next, all subjects listened to "one of the most worthless and uninteresting discussions imaginable." Afterward, they rated the discussion and its participants. High scores indicate a favorable attitude. The means, an ANOVA summary table, and two HSD values are shown. Write an interpretation of these results.

	Severe Embarrassment	Mild Embarrassment	No Embarrassment
Group Means	195.3	171.1	166.7

Source	df	MS	F
Between Groups	2	124.60	5.75
Within Groups	57	21.67	
Total	59		

HSD (severe vs. mild) = 4.50;

HSD (mild vs. no) = 1.38

3. A vintner wanted to market a new white wine that would be a blend of several varietals grown in his vineyards. He developed four blends, and he wanted to decide which was the best. He employed the services of eight wine tasters and had them rate each of the four wines on a 7-point scale, ranging from abominable (1) to exquisite (7). Explain why the ANOVA method described in Chapter 9 is inappropriate for the analysis of the data.

PROBLEMS

1. As you know from the text, the time required to extinguish a response depends on the schedule of reinforcement during learning. It also depends on the predictability of the reinforcement. The following data are patterned after Hulse (1973) who reported on the effects of predictability. In this study all the pigeons pecked an average of four times for each reinforcement, but the predictability of a reinforcement varied for the three groups. The Very Predictable group was on an FR4 schedule--every fourth response was reinforced. (This is one of the schedules used in the text problem.) The Fairly Predictable group got a reinforcement after two, then

four, then six responses. The pattern then repeated. The Unpredictable group was on a schedule produced by a random number generator. It was programmed, however, so that on the average, every fourth response was reinforced. (The name of this schedule is variable ratio-4, abbreviated as VR4.) After ten days of training on their schedule, extinction began (responses were never again reinforced.) The time to extinction is shown. Analyze the data as completely as you can and write a conclusion about the predictability of reinforcement and persistence.

Very Predictable	Fairly Predictable	Unpredictable
8	16	18
13	11	19
11	15	22
8		16
		15

2. A clinical psychologist at a Veterans Hospital investigated the phenomenon that Viet Nam veterans fail to respond to traditional therapy. He hypothesized that guilt feelings associated with participation in a war they did not believe in were responsible. As a partial test of his hypothesis, he conducted a standardized interview with four groups of veterans: a WW II group, a Korean group, a Viet Nam group that was hospitalized, and a Viet Nam group that was functioning normally. The dependent variable was the number of statements that reflected personal guilt. Analyze the data with an ANOVA and any Tukey HSD tests that are appropriate.

WW II	Korean	Viet Nam Hospitalized	Viet Nam Normal
2	7	9	7
5	4	7	3
7	9	12	10
2	4	12	8

3. In most hospital delivery rooms, an evaluation is made of the well-being of newborn infants at one minute of age and again at five minutes of age. The scale used is the Apgar Scale, which uses certain criteria to rate the infant's heart rate, respiratory effort, crying, muscle tone, and color. Scale values are 0, 1, or 2, with 2 being the best rating. The overall score is the sum of five ratings. Thus, scores from 0–10 are possible, with 10 indicating the highest general well-being. Suppose a developmental psychologist obtained permission from a large hospital to be present in the delivery room and to rate newborn infants on the Apgar Scale. The independent variable of interest to her was the type of anesthetic given to the mother. Four types were included: twilight sleep induced by sedatives, the spinal block, the pudendal local anesthetic, and the Lamaze method of natural childbirth with no drugs used. The psychologist suspected that the sedatives used to produce twilight sleep might be harmful to the child because they passed the placental barrier and entered the child's bloodstream. She also thought that babies born by the Lamaze method might experience less trauma and thus score higher on the Apgar Scale. Below are summary data for the five-minute Apgar scores for the newborns. Perform an ANOVA and make any appropriate HSD tests. Write an interpretation for the results.

	Twilight	Spinal	Pudendal	Lamaze
ΣX	49	74	78	83
ΣX^2	269	574	636	711
N	10	10	10	10

4. A political scientist surveyed attitudes of the citizens of a town of 12,000 toward their city government. Below are the scores of three groups of citizens. Perform an ANOVA and explain the results. (Higher scores mean more positive attitudes.)

Business Owners and Managers (X_1)	Blue Collar Workers (X_2)	Laborers (X_3)
18	18	15
17	16	14
16	15	14
16	15	13
15	14	13
14	14	12
14	12	11
13	11	10
9	9	8
	7	6
	6	4
	3	2

CHAPTER 10   ANALYSIS OF VARIANCE: FACTORIAL DESIGN

SUMMARY

The factorial design described in Chapter 10 is one with two independent variables (factors). Every level of one variable is paired with every level of the other variable. Thus, each subject in the experiment can be classified in two ways--once according to one independent variable and a second time according to the other independent variable. This is illustrated in Table 10.1. The group of subjects in the upper left-hand cell of the table get Level 1 of A and Level 1 of B.

Table 10.1.   Illustration of a Factorial Design

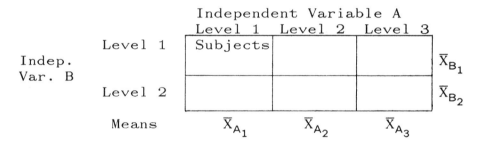

Table 10.1 also shows the means for two of the three statistical tests that are run on a factorial design. One is a comparison between $\overline{X}_{B_1}$ and $\overline{X}_{B_2}$, the means of the two levels of independent variable B. The second test is a comparison of the means, $\overline{X}_{A_1}$, $\overline{X}_{A_2}$, and $\overline{X}_{A_3}$, the three levels of the other independent variable. Both of these tests are called main effects and each is comparable to a one-way ANOVA like that of Chapter 9. The third test in a factorial ANOVA is for an interaction between the two

independent variables. Interactions occur when the effect of changing levels in one independent variable depends upon which level of the other independent variable you are administering.

Perhaps an example of a significant interaction will help you with the concept of an interaction. The effect of chilling a rat until its body temperature is 20°C (37°C is normal) is disastrous; the rat dies. Likewise, asphyxiating a rat causes death. What chance would you predict for a rat undergoing asphyxiation while its body temperature is lowered to 20°C? The usual prediction is (death)^2. In this case, however, there is an interaction; the rat lives for a very long time under these conditions. Each condition separately would kill the animal, but together they do not kill.*

In Table 10.2 we have cast this fact in terms of a 2 × 2 factorial design.

Table 10.2. Illustration of a Significant Interaction

| | | Body Temperature | |
		37°C	20°C
	No	Alive	Dead
Asphyxiation			
	Yes	Dead	Alive

The effect of changing from 37°C to 20°C depends on whether or not the animal is being asphyxiated. If the animal is not being asphyxiated, changing from 37°C to 20°C kills it. If the animal is being asphyxiated, the effect is just the opposite; changing from 37°C to 20°C restores life. To sum up, there is significant interaction in Table 10.2; the effect of asphyxiation depends on body temperature.

*Asphyxiation-hypothermia experiments on rats and guinea pigs were carried out because hypothermia appears to save newborn human infants whose respiration does not begin within a very few minutes after birth.

If you obtain one or two significant main effects in a factorial experiment and if the interaction is not significant, you may make comparisons among the means to find out which ones are significantly different from the others. As in Chapter 9, a post hoc test, Tukey's HSD, may be used to make all possible pairwise comparisons.

MULTIPLE-CHOICE QUESTIONS

1. As used in analysis of variance, the term factor means

    (1) independent variable;
    (2) dependent variable;
    (3) extraneous variable;
    (4) none of the above.

2. In a factorial ANOVA, a cell is

    (1) one level of the independent variable;
    (2) one level of the dependent variable;
    (3) one level of one independent variable and one level of a second independent variable;
    (4) all the subjects in the experiment.

3. Designs that are equal in the number of factors are

    (1) independent t test and factorial ANOVA;
    (2) correlated t test and factorial ANOVA;
    (3) one-way ANOVA and factorial ANOVA;
    (4) none of the above.

4. A social psychologist was interested in the effect of propaganda on attitudes of males and females. He measured attitudes toward democracy for all subjects, delivered the propaganda, and remeasured attitudes toward democracy. He wanted to analyze the data using a 2 x 2 factorial with sex as one independent variable and before-and-after

94

attitudes as the other. The techniques presented in the text will not permit this because

(1) the scores are not independent;
(2) an independent variable was not defined;
(3) the dependent variable was not defined;
(4) the levels of the independent variable were not chosen at random by the experimenter.

5. When the cell means of a factorial design are graphed, an insignificant interaction is indicated by

(1) parallel lines;
(2) crossed lines;
(3) values of F less than 1.00;
(4) any of the above.

6. Which of the following is <u>not</u> a restriction placed on the factorial analysis described in Chapter 10?

(1) Scores must be independent.
(2) Levels of the independent variable must be chosen by the experimenter.
(3) The number of degrees of freedom must be large.
(4) The number of scores in each cell must be equal.

7. In a 4 x 4 factorial design with five subjects per cell, the df for the interaction F would be

(1) 3, 70 df;
(2) 6, 64 df;
(3) 9, 64 df;
(4) none of the above.

8. The term <u>main effect</u> refers to a com-
    parison of

    (1) means; *marginal*
    (2) interactions;
    (3) both of the above;
    (4) neither of the above.

9. Mr. Brown, a farmer-philosopher, grows
    corn. On his fields 5-10-5 fertilizer
    (5 percent nitrogen, 10 percent potash,
    5 percent potassium) causes a 10 percent
    increase in yield of corn. 10-20-10 fer-
    tilizer causes a 15 percent increase in
    yield of corn. Suppose both fertilizers
    were applied by Brown (whose philosophy is,
    "If a little bit does a little good, a
    whole lot will do a whole lot of good.").
    Which outcome below would be true if there
    were no interaction?

    (1) 10 percent increase;
    (2) 15 percent increase;
    (3) either (1) or (2);
    (4) 25 percent increase.

10. "The means of the populations from which
    the samples were drawn are identical."
    This is a statement of

    (1) the null hypothesis;
    (2) one of the assumptions required of
         data that are subjected to a factorial
         ANOVA;
    (3) both of the above;
    (4) neither of the above.

11. Which of the following is true?

    (1) $df_A + df_B = df_{AB}$;
    (2) $MS_A + MS_B = MS_{AB}$;
    (3) both of the above;
    (4) neither of the above.

12. In common with one-way ANOVA, factorial ANOVA has the following restrictions and limitations:

    (1) the dependent variable is assumed to be normally distributed;
    (2) the population variances of all the populations sampled are equal;
    (3) both of the above;
    (4) neither of the above.

13. Consider a factorial ANOVA in which the dependent variable is reaction time scores. Three different drugs are tested on both females and males. The researchers concluded that the effect of a drug did not depend on whether the person taking it was a female or male. The factorial ANOVA would certainly show that

    (1) there is no main effect for drug;
    (2) there is no main effect for gender;
    (3) there is no interaction;
    (4) all of the above.

14. Suppose a 4 × 5 factorial ANOVA with six scores per cell produced a $MS_B = 49$ and a $MS_{wg} = 20$. (B is the 5 in the 4 × 5.) With respect to Tukey's HSD, which of the following is true at the .05 level? Tukey's HSD

    (1) is not appropriate in this instance;
    (2) would call a difference between two means of 7.50 significant;
    (3) would call a difference between two means of 7.10 significant;
    (4) both (2) and (3).

INTERPRETATION

1. A nursing home superintendent was concerned about the spatial disorientation exhibited by some of the residents. Though they had been in the home for several years, they

97

had difficulty locating their rooms, the dining hall, the lounge, and so on--a common problem with the elderly in nursing homes. She devised a program of Spatial Orientation Therapy, which she felt might help such patients, and decided to put it to a statistical test. She felt that the program might differ in its effects on patients who were mobile and patients who were confined to wheelchairs. She randomly selected 16 wheelchair patients and 16 mobile patients who were described by the nursing staff as disoriented. Half of the patients in each group were randomly selected to receive the therapy program, with the other half serving as controls. The nursing staff, unaware of the therapy program, was instructed to record instances of disorientation on all 32 patients over a one-week period after therapy was completed. Below is a table of cell means and a summary table of the ANOVA. Write a conclusion for the study.

		Therapy A_1	Control A_2
Mobility (B)	Wheel-chair (B_1)	9.625	13.125
	Mobile (B_2)	6.000	9.875

Source	df	SS	MS	F
A (Treatment)	1	108.7812	108.7812	5.44
B (Mobility)	1	94.5312	94.5312	4.73
AB	1	.2816	.2816	0.01
Within Groups	28	559.6250	19.9866	
Total	31	763.2188		

People who have therapy

$p > .05$

98

The affects of therapy doesn't depend on mobility of resident
don't draw graph

2. Milton Rokeach has proposed that racial and ethnic prejudice occurs, not because of differences in race and ethnicity, but because people assume that there are also differences in basic values. Studies similar to the following have been done to test Rokeach's hypothesis. Three groups of subjects are chosen on the basis of their scores on a "prejudice" test. One group has low prejudice scores; one, moderate scores; and one, high scores. All subjects read descriptions of three people. Half of the subjects in each prejudice group read descriptions of people who differed from them in values but not in race. The other half read descriptions of people who differed from them in race but not in values. Subjects indicated, on a 7-point scale, the degree of intimacy they were willing to display toward each person described. The highest intimacy was indicated by 7, and the lowest intimacy by 1. Analyze the data from this experiment, and use the results to comment on Rokeach's hypothesis. (The dependent variable is the total "intimacy" score assigned to three described people.) The cell means and a source table are shown.

| | Prejudice (A) | | |
	Low (A_1)	Moderate (A_2)	High (A_1)
Different in Values (B_1)	8.20	9.00	10.40
Different in Race (B_2)	15.40	13.40	7.00

Source	df	SS	MS	F	p
Prejudice (A)	2	54.0667	27.0334	7.5092	<.01
Difference (B)	1	56.0334	56.0334	15.5648	<.01
AB	2	150.8667	75.4334	20.9537	<.01

99

Source	df	SS	MS	F	p
Within groups	24	86.40		3.60	
Total	29				

3. A social psychologist wanted to investigate the effect of physical attractiveness on how people evaluate each other. She selected 60 undergraduate students, 30 males and 30 females, as subjects. Each subject conducted a telephone conversation with an opposite-sexed person and then made an evaluation of the person "as a person" on a 10-point scale. Before each conversation, the subject was given a description of the person who would be on the telephone line. The descriptions included "truly gorgeous," "kind of ordinary looking," or "ugly as a mud fence." In fact, all male subjects talked to the same female, and all female subjects talked to the same male. Analyze the following summary tables, and use the results to discuss the effect of perceived physical appearance on the evaluation of others "as people."

Cell Means

	Males (A_1)	Females (A_2)
Gorgeous (B_1)	8.10	8.00
Ordinary (B_2)	6.10	6.50
Ugly (B_3)	4.60	4.70

Source	df	SS	MS	F	p
Gender (A)	1	.2666	.2666	0.09	>.05
Description (B)	2	115.6333	57.8167	18.50	<.01
AB	2	.6334	.3167	0.10	>.05
Within Groups	54	168.80	3.1259		
Total	59	285.3333			

1. John McCullers contends that providing material rewards for performing tasks may impair intrinsic motivation and cause a dislike for the task. A test of this idea might be carried out with an experiment like the following. Select a task to be performed--say, washing a stack of dirty dishes. Have a group of people rate their attitudes toward washing dishes on a 7-point scale--ranging from 1 for "detest" to 7 for "enjoy." Select as subjects for the experiment the eight people with the highest scores and the eight with the lowest scores (low and high below). Half the people in each group are promised (and paid) money for washing dishes. The other half are thanked. Following the dishwashing task (and payment or "thank you"), the subjects again rate their attitudes toward washing dishes. We have no idea what the results of such an experiment would be, but assume that the following rating scores are collected after the task. Analyze the data, and use the results to comment on McCullers' notion.

1 effect

Attitude Toward Washing Dishes
(Before Task)

	Low	High
	4	7
	3	6
Money	3	5
	2	5
	5	7
	3	6
"Thanks"	2	6
	1	5

2. Carl Hovland (Hovland, Lumsdaine, & Shef-field, 1949) conducted a study during WW II to find out whether people were more likely to be persuaded by a message that gave just one side of an issue or by one that gave both sides. (In 1944, Germany was falling, and the attitude of many American soldiers was that the war with Japan would soon be over. Afraid that battle preparedness would fall off, the Army wanted to reverse this attitude. The question was "How should we present the argument?") In one part of Hovland's study, there were two independent vari-ables--number of sides of the argument pre-sented and educational level of the listeners. The dependent variable was the amount of attitude change produced. Below are summary data. Finish the analysis, and interpret the results.

	High School Graduate	
	Yes (A_1)	No (A_2)
One-sided (B_1)	$\Sigma X_{A_1B_1} = 64$ $\Sigma X^2_{A_1B_1} = 808$ $N = 6$	$\Sigma X_{A_2B_1} = 123$ $\Sigma X^2_{A_2B_1} = 2603$ $N = 6$
Two-sided (B_2)	$\Sigma X_{A_1B_2} = 114$ $\Sigma X^2_{A_1B_2} = 2218$ $N = 6$	$\Sigma X_{A_2B_2} = 62$ $\Sigma X^2_{A_2B_2} = 670$ $N = 6$

(Argument is the row label spanning B_1 and B_2.)

3. This problem is based on an interesting and important study done by Temerlin (1968). In his study, a taped interview with a "completely normal man" was presented to several groups of clinical psychologists, psychiatrists, and graduate students in clinical psychology. For some groups, the interview was portrayed as an employment interview. For some, it was portrayed as

102

a diagnostic interview where information was "accidentally" released that "this is a completely normal man." For others, the information was that "he may look neurotic but actually is quite psychotic." Those viewing the tape rated the man in the interview on a 10-point scale from 1 (completely normal) to 10 (severely disturbed). N = 6 for each cell. Analyze the data including HSD tests. Analyzed correctly, your conclusions will be similar to those found by Temerlin.

		Information (Factor A)		
		Employment Interview (A_1)	Diagnostic Interview (A_2) "Normal"	Diagnostic Interview (A_3) "Psychotic"
Diagnostician (Factor B)	Clin. Psy. (B_1)	$\Sigma X_{A_1B_1} = 16$ $\Sigma X^2_{A_1B_1} = 56$	$\Sigma X_{A_2B_1} = 11$ $\Sigma X^2_{A_2B_1} = 25$	$\Sigma X_{A_3B_1} = 46$ $\Sigma X^2_{A_3B_1} = 360$
	Psych. (B_2)	$\Sigma X_{A_1B_2} = 15$ $\Sigma X^2_{A_1B_2} = 43$	$\Sigma X_{A_2B_2} = 11$ $\Sigma X^2_{A_2B_2} = 23$	$\Sigma X_{A_3B_3} = 43$ $\Sigma X^2_{A_3B_2} = 329$
	Grad. Stud. (B_3)	$\Sigma X_{A_1B_3} = 15$ $\Sigma X^2_{A_1B_3} = 47$	$\Sigma X_{A_2B_3} = 10$ $\Sigma X^2_{A_2B_3} = 20$	$\Sigma X_{A_3B_3} = 43$ $\Sigma X^2_{A_3B_3} = 331$

CHAPTER 11   THE CHI SQUARE DISTRIBUTION

SUMMARY

Chi square (χ^2) is an inferential statis- tics technique that is used when <u>sample</u> data are reported as frequencies. Chi square compares these observed frequencies to expected frequen- cies that are produced by a hypothesis about the <u>population</u> of data. There are two possible out- comes of this comparison.

1.   The hypothesis about the population is supported. (Chance alone could account for the differences between the observed frequencies and those predicted by the hypothesis.)

2.   The hypothesis about the population is rejected. (The probability is low that the difference between the observed fre- quencies and those predicted by the hypothesis are due to chance.)

Two kinds of χ^2 tests were described in this chapter. In a test of <u>goodness of fit</u>, the hypothesis about the population is a theory. If the null hypothesis is retained (outcome 1 above), the theory is supported by the data. If the null hypothesis is rejected (outcome 2), the theory has failed.
In a test of <u>independence</u>, the hypothesis about the population is that the two variables under consideration are independent. If the null hypothesis is retained (outcome 1), the hypothesis of independence is supported. If the null hypothesis is rejected (outcome 2), you can conclude that the two variables are related; they are not independent.

One section in this chapter deals with the problems of small <u>expected</u> frequencies in a cell. The best solution is to avoid the problem by having large N's. A second solution is to combine categories, which results in fewer categories and larger expected frequencies.

Three methods of determining degrees of freedom were described. Number of categories minus one is appropriate for goodness-of-fit tests when there is one variable with two or more categories and when the only restriction is that $\Sigma E = \Sigma O$. If other restrictions are added (for example, that the mean and standard deviation of the expected scores be a particular value), one df is subtracted for each parameter estimated. Finally, df = $(R - 1)(C - 1)$ is appropriate for tests with two variables.

Chi square, which is an invention of Karl Pearson, requires data in the form of frequency counts. Each event must be independent of the others. Like the other inferential statistics you have studied, the data you analyze should be representative of (perhaps even a random sample of) the population you are interested in.

MULTIPLE-CHOICE QUESTIONS

1. The person who developed χ^2 was

    (1)   Ronald A. Fisher;
    (2)   William S. Gosset;
    (3)   Karl Pearson;
    (4)   Helen Walker.

2. The shape of the theoretical χ^2 distribution is determined by

    (1)   the number of observations;
    (2)   the size of the expected frequency of events;
    (3)   the number of categories of events;
    (4)   all of the above.

3. The sum of the expected frequencies must be equal to

    (1) the sum of the observed frequencies;
    (2) the df;
    (3) $(R - 1)(C - 1)$;
    (4) none of the above.

4. A developmental psychologist developed a theory that predicted the proportion of children who would, in a period of stress, cling to the mother, attack the mother, or attack a younger sibling. The stress situation was set up, and the responses of 50 children were recorded. The appropriate χ^2 test is a test of

    (1) goodness of fit with 2 df;
    (2) goodness of fit with 40 df;
    (3) independence with 2 df;
    (4) independence with 40 df.

5. The null hypothesis for a goodness-of-fit test is that the observed frequencies

    (1) fit the expected frequencies;
    (2) do not fit the expected frequencies;
    (3) either of the above, depending on the size of the χ^2 value;
    (4) either of the above, depending on the size of the χ^2 and the df.

6. In a χ^2 test of independence between sex and kinds of phobias, the null hypothesis was rejected. The proper conclusion is that

    (1) sex and phobias are independent of each other;
    (2) sex and phobias are related to each other;
    (3) knowing a person's phobia gives you no clue to his or her sex;
    (4) none of the above.

7. A χ^2 test of goodness of fit was used to evaluate a model. The null hypothesis was rejected. The proper conclusion is that the model is

    (1) adequate;
    (2) inadequate;
    (3) either (1) or (2), depending on the df;
    (4) models must be evaluated with a test of independence.

8. In order to use the chi square distribution with confidence you must assume that the observations you make

    (1) are normally distributed;
    (2) have equal variance;
    (3) are independent;
    (4) all of the above.

9. To find expected frequencies in a test of independence,

    (1) begin by assuming that the categories of events are independent;
    (2) use predictions based on a theory;
    (3) begin by assuming that the categories of events are related in some way;
    (4) none of the above.

10. Rejection of the null hypothesis for a test of independence is to rejection of the null hypothesis for a goodness-of-fit test as

    (1) independence is to retention of the model;
    (2) independence is to rejection of the model;
    (3) dependence is to retention of the model;
    (4) dependence is to rejection of the model.

11. Suppose you were analyzing data from a 2 × 2 test of independence and you had one expected frequency that was very small. According to your text you are very likely to make a

(1) Type I error;
(2) Type II error;
(3) both of the above;
(4) neither of the above.

12. If you compare chi square curves for skewness you'll find that as degrees of freedom increase the curves are

(1) positively skewed but becoming less so;
(2) positively skewed and becoming more so;
(3) negatively skewed and becoming less so;
(4) negatively skewed and becoming more so.

13. Historically, chi square came along about the same time as

(1) the normal curve;
(2) the correlation coefficient;
(3) analysis of variance;
(4) Arabic numbers.

INTERPRETATION

1. In the study of human origins, anthropologists divide themselves into two camps: the "lumpers" (who argue that all the pieces of evidence are not that different) and the "splitters" (who argue that the differences represent separate species). A budding anthropologist wondered if being a lumper or splitter was related to experience as an anthropologist. She gathered the following data, which produced a χ^2 value of 16.67.

108

What conclusion about anthropologists is appropriate?

	Lumpers	Splitters	
≤ 5 yrs. experience	10	30	40
> 5 yrs. experience	40	20	60
	50	50	

2. A small college was intent on obtaining a more geographically diverse student body. Most of its students came from the surrounding five-county area. The admissions staff asked graduates outside this area and outside the state to help with recruiting. In addition, some money was spent on media advertising. To assess the effect of this campaign, the current year's requests for applications were classified as: five-county area (565), rest of state (410), and out of state (216). An analysis of addresses over previous years showed: five-county area (51%), rest of state (40%), and out of state (9%). A χ^2 analysis produced the following table. Examine it, decide whether this is a test of independence or a goodness-of-fit test, and tell the story that the data support.

0	E	(0 - E)	(0 - E)^2	$\dfrac{(0 - E)^2}{E}$
565	607.4	-42.40	1797.76	2.96
410	476.4	-66.40	4408.96	9.25
216	107.2	108.80	11837.44	110.42
			$\chi^2 =$	122.64

3. Fred Stodtbeck (1951) carried out a study of family decision making in two different cultures: the Navaho, which is matrilineal, and the Mormon, which is patrilineal. A matrilineal culture is one in which the

109

prestige of kinship or material support of the family belongs primarily to the wife. In a patrilineal culture, this prestige belongs to the husband. In Stodtbeck's study of the Navaho culture, husbands won 34 decisions and the wives won 46. Among the Mormons, the husbands won 42 decisions, and the wives 29. A χ^2 analysis produced a χ^2 value of 4.17. Tell the story.

PROBLEMS

1. In an activity-wheel experiment, animals were either isolated or housed together. Both groups were allowed food for one hour each day. After 25 days, the animals were either alive with stabilized weights or they were dead. Test for the independence of these two conditions with a χ^2 test. Write a conclusion. For the reasoning behind this experiment, see Spatz and Jones (1971).

| | Living Conditions | |
	Isolated	Together
Alive	9	8
Dead	1	12

2. With tomatoes, the color of the fruit and the height of the plant are genetically determined (with red dominant over yellow, and tall dominant over short). Suppose for a few minutes that you were a geneticist during the 1920s or 1930s when these facts were unknown. If the above facts about dominance are true, a particular set of crossings will result in a 9:3:3:1 ratio, with 9 tall reds to 3 short reds to 3 tall yellows to 1 short yellow. Suppose you carried out the crossings and found 90 tall reds, 39 short reds, 39 tall yellows, and 18 short yellows. Use a χ^2 test to deter-determine if such data fit a 9:3:3:1 model. (Note: 9:3:3:1 is a shortcut way to write $\frac{9}{16}$, $\frac{3}{16}$, $\frac{3}{16}$, $\frac{1}{16}$.) Is this a test for inde-pendence or goodness of fit?

110

3. Due to the long-term popularity of movies,
    books, and TV programs dealing with space
    travel and alien beings, a researcher
    became interested in the degree to which
    people believed in alien life. In particu-
    lar, he wondered if the degree of belief
    was related to level of education. He did
    a study in which he asked 173 people to
    respond to the statement "Our planet is
    being observed by intelligent life forms
    from outer space." Responses were given on
    a 7-point scale from "Strong Agreement" to
    "Strong Disagreement." The number of peo-
    ple responding in each category is given
    below. Analyze the data, and comment on
    the relationship between level of education
    and agreement with the statement.

Level of Agreement	College Educated	High School Dropouts
Strong Agreement	2	4
Mild Agreement	7	10
Slight Agreement	15	24
Neutral	19	21
Slight Disagreement	23	18
Mild Disagreement	12	9
Strong Disagreement	6	3

4. A highway engineer predicted that the per-
    centage of vehicles in the following weight
    categories would be observed if a new
    bridge was completed. He based these pre-
    dictions on guesses about increased manu-
    facturing in the area served by the
    highway.

Up to 4500 pounds	47%
4501 to 6000	30%
6001 to 10,000	15%
10,000 up	8%

The bridge was built and during a test period the following vehicle observations were made. Write a conclusion about the engineer's predictions and indicate which of the two kinds of chi square tests is being performed on the data.

Up to 4500 pounds	155
4501 to 6000	82
6001 to 10,000	37
10,001 up	32

CHAPTER 12   NONPARAMETRIC STATISTICS

SUMMARY

Four nonparametric statistical methods are
described in this chapter. They are the Mann-
Whitney U test, the Wilcoxon matched-pairs
signed-ranks test, the Wilcoxon-Wilcox multiple-
comparisons test, and Spearman's r_s. These
methods all reduce the observations to ranks,
and the statistical operations are performed on
the ranks.

All four of these methods use the hypothe-
sis-testing procedures you have been working
with since Chapter 7 ("Differences between
Means"). For the first three of these methods,
the hypothesis being tested is that the samples
came from populations that had identical distributions. For the fourth method, r_s (a descriptive statistic) is calculated, then the
hypothesis tested is that the sample r_s came
from a bivariate population with a correlation
of .00.

The Mann-Whitney U test is used to determine if two independent samples came from the
same population. The Wilcoxon matched-pairs
signed-ranks test is used to determine if two
correlated samples came from the same population. The Wilcoxon-Wilcox multiple-comparisons
test is used to test for differences between all
possible pairs of independent, equal-sized
samples.

These three methods are used instead of a t
test or an ANOVA if the data are ranks. In
addition, many researchers will use them when
the populations are not normally distributed or
the populations do not have equal variances.

1. The nonparametric tests in the text are based on sampling distributions of

   (1) means;
   (2) mean differences;
   (3) ranks;
   (4) variances.

2. The nonparametric test that corresponds in design to the independent-samples t test is the

   (1) Mann-Whitney U test;
   (2) Wilcoxon matched-pairs signed-ranks test;
   (3) Wilcoxon-Wilcox multiple-comparisons test;
   (4) r_s.

3. Suppose you find that three people tied for the top score in a Wilcoxon-Wilcox multiple comparisons test. The correct procedure is to

   (1) assign a rank of 1 to all three;
   (2) assign a rank of 2 to all three;
   (3) assign a rank of 3 to all three;
   (4) randomly determine which scores get ranks 1, 2, and 3.

4. Nonparametric tests are used rather than a t test or an ANOVA when

   (1) the researcher does not know the specific value of the population parameters;
   (2) the data are in the form of ranks;
   (3) the assumption of random sampling is not justified;
   (4) both (2) and (3).

5. The null hypothesis for testing the significance of r_s is that the population rho is equal to

(1)   .00;
(2)   1.00;
(3)   the statistic, rho, based on the sample data;
(4)   none of the above.

6. The name(s) used for the tests presented in Chapter 12 is (are)

    (1)   nonparametric;
    (2)   distribution free;
    (3)   assumption free r;
    (4)   all of the above.

7. When sample size is large, a U from a Mann-Whitney U test can be evaluated by using

    (1)   a t distribution;
    (2)   the normal distribution;
    (3)   an F distribution;
    (4)   a χ^2 distribution.

8. To test for a significant difference between correlated samples, you should use a

    (1)   Mann-Whitney U test;
    (2)   Wilcoxon matched-pairs signed-ranks test;
    (3)   Wilcoxon-Wilcox multiple-comparisons test;
    (4) r_s.

9. Which of the following could not be analyzed with a Wilcoxon-Wilcox multiple-comparisons test?

    (1)   three independent samples;
    (2) $N_1 = 10$, $N_2 = 20$, $N_3 = 30$;
    (3)   the data for the three groups consisting of ranks in college;
    (4)   all of the above.

10. What rank would a score of 4 have on the following distribution?

1, 2, 2, 3, 3, 4, 4, 5, 5.

(1) 4;
(2) 5.5;
(3) 6;
(4) 7;
(5) none of the above, answer is _____.

11. Power is the likelihood of

(1) rejecting H_0 when it is true;
(1) rejecting H_0 when it is false;
(3) retaining H_0 when it is true;
(4) retaining H_0 when it is false.

12. Suppose you found, for the 26 people in your wing of the dorm, a Spearman's r_s of .38 between the number of breakfasts eaten during the term and grade point average. You may conclude that there is

(1) no significant relationship;
(2) a significant relationship at the .05 level;
(3) a significant relationship at the .01 level;
(4) a significant relationship at the .001 level.

13. If you have one difference score of 0 it should be kept in the analysis for

(1) Wilcoxon matched-pairs signed-ranks test;
(2) Spearman's r_s;
(3) both of the above;
(4) neither of the above.

14. _____ require that the samples be selected randomly from the populations in question

(1) parametric tests;
(2) nonparametric tests;
(3) both of the above;
(4) neither of the above.

INTERPRETATION

1. Which nonparametric test should be used to analyze data from the following studies?

   A. Some experimenters, impressed by the effectiveness of a steady, direct gaze by dominant primates, decided to investigate the effect in <u>Homo sapiens</u>. They rode a motor scooter up next to a car stopped at an intersection with a stoplight and either stared directly at the driver or stared ahead. The dependent variable was the time it took the driver to cross the intersection. (Results: staring increases speed for <u>Homo sapiens</u> too.)

   B. Countries are ranked on infant mortality rates. Suppose you had the ranks for 15 countries and you also had the rank for each of the countries on population density. What would you do to find whether there was a relationship between the two variables?

   C. To determine if there was sex discrimination on salaries at Whassamatter U., a statistician began with 15 female professors. Each was matched with a male professor for degree, discipline, and years of experience.

   D. High-frustration subjects were forced to wait for a late participant for 15 minutes before beginning an experiment. Low-frustration subjects started on time. During the experiment aggression was measured as the dependent variable.

   E. To gather information to decide whether "Small is Beautiful" or "Bigger is Better," a student calculated the average student enrollment: Small, Medium, Large, Giant. The average student rating was converted to a rank for each of the 20.

   F. In a before-and-after study with a propaganda movie in between, participants rated their views on abortion.

117

2. A practical question facing most students is how to most efficiently use the study time available (that is, how to have more time to play). Gates conducted an early study (1917), which we have used as a model for the data that follow. Twenty students were divided into five groups. The students studied an article on dinosaurs, and each group spent a different proportion of the total study time in "self-recitation" (looking away from the article and mentally reciting what had been learned). Afterward, each student took a 100-point test on the material in the article. The sums of the ranks are shown below. (The best score was ranked 1.) Finish the analysis and write an explanation that the data support.

Proportion of Study Time
Spent in Self-Recitation

0	20	40	60	80
73	54	44.5	27.5	11

3. A P.E. instructor designed a CVR (cardio-vascular-respiratory) fitness program that involved gradually increasing the duration and intensity of exercise over a six-month period. The participants in the program were measured for general fitness at the beginning and at the end of the program on such measures as percent body fat, vital lung capacity, and blood pressure and heart rate before and after exercise. Each participant was assigned a "fitness" score on a scale of 1 (a physical disaster) to 10 (a superb specimen). A t value of 5.5 was found when a Wilcoxon matched-pairs signed-ranks test was run. Was the program effective in improving CVR fitness?

4. A social psychologist wanted to test the assertion that "too much sexual knowledge at too early an age will result in promiscuity." This argument is often used in opposition to the offering of sex education

118

in the public schools. She randomly selected 25 college sophomore women, asked them if they had a sex education course in elementary school, and then asked them to complete a questionnaire concerning their sexual activity. Two refused to complete the questionnaire. She then used the questionnaire results to rank-order the women from most (rank = 1) to least (rank = 23) sexually active. The sum of ranks for those who had not had a sex education course (N = 14) was 135. For those who had taken a course (N = 9), the sum was 141. The smaller U value was 30. Complete the analysis and comment on the assertion.

5. Work Problem 1 that follows and then come back to this interpretation problem.

Besides tests that were chosen to simulate pilots' eye-hand coordination tasks, printed tests were used. A Spearman's rho between a general information test (name the five Great Lakes) and the pilot competency test was .49. Compare this correlation coefficient to that in Problem 1 and draw a conclusion.

PROBLEMS

1. During WW II, enlistees were selected for pilot training on the basis of test scores. Some of the tests were printed, and some were eye-hand coordination tests chosen to simulate tasks that pilots actually performed. One popular eye-hand coordination test was the pursuit rotor. The data that follow show time on target for the pursuit rotor during the fifth trial of practice and a "pilot competency score," based on actual flying skill. Find r_s (which will be the same as that found by Air Force researchers).

Seconds on Target Max. = 30	Pilot Competency Score
18	37
15	57
28	63
25	41
9	31
17	51
23	42
11	45

2. A consulting firm wanted to sell a large manufacturing company a sensitivity training workshop for their supervisors. The sales pitch was that, if supervisors were more sensitive to the feelings of the employees, they would be better liked and that this improved rapport would increase productivity. Because of the high cost for the training program, the plant manager insisted on a test. Eight supervisors were randomly selected. Four of them received the sensitivity training program, whereas the other four didn't. The output of the eight supervisors was then ranked with the following results. Should the company buy the training program?

Rank of Supervisor	Training Program
1	yes
2	no
3	no
4	yes
5	yes
6	yes
7	no
8	no

3. Many nurses, like most other people, are reluctant to approach patients diagnosed as having psychological problems. This reluctance causes problems in providing fully adequate hospital care for such patients. To help alleviate the problem, a Director of Nursing contracted with a local community mental health agency to provide an in-service training program to change nurses' attitudes toward such patients. To assess the effectiveness of the program, two matched groups were formed. One group completed the program, and both groups were given an attitude test. Higher scores indicate more positive attitudes toward patients with psychological problems. Analyze the data with a Wilcoxon matched-pairs signed-ranks test, and comment on the success or failure of the program.

| | Attitude Scores | |
Matched Pairs	Untrained	Trained
1	21	23
2	12	18
3	17	22
4	23	23
5	16	17
6	21	24
7	19	27
8	14	13

4. A consumer advocate wanted to compare the cleanliness of four chains of supermarkets. He devised a 50-point rating scale to be used in the inspection of six stores of each chain. The higher the score, the cleaner the store. Analyze the data, and make your shopping recommendations to the public.

Score	Chain	Score	Chain	Score	Chain
35	A	49	D	47	C
39	C	27	B	44	A
29	B	31	B	48	D
43	C	46	A	28	B
50	D	34	B	37	A
26	A	42	C	36	C
41	C	32	D	45	D
33	D	38	A	40	B

APPENDIX: ARITHMETIC AND ALGEBRA REVIEW

SUMMARY

This chapter affects different students in different ways. For some, most of the chapter is worthless; these students remember all the arithmetic and algebra perfectly well. For many, it is helpful; students are glad to brush up on a few rusty skills. For a few, it is a most helpful chapter; the students never learned the arithmetic and algebra, and they don't have the background to continue, and this chapter persuades them to drop the course. If you are in the large, middle group, you should mark in your textbook those sections in which you missed problems, find the corresponding section below, and work the problems. For practice in rounding off numbers, work the section on decimals.

The symbols at the end of the textbook chapter involve simple memorization. Although not a very satisfactory kind of learning, memorization will pay off when these symbols are introduced again in the following two chapters.

PROBLEMS

Decimals (Round all answers to three decimal places, if rounding is necessary.)

Add:

    1. $4.68 + 8 + 2.163 + 1.0005$

    2. $185 + .185 + 1.85 + 18.5$

    3. $22.06 + 2.534 + .0602 + 10.003$

    4. $5.2 + 12 + 9.74$

Subtract:

    5. 456.217 - 82.4   7. 89 - 23.72

    6. 1.0 - .38751   8. .0456 - .0079

Multiply: Divide:

    9. 5.32 × 2   13. 6.82 ÷ 1.3

   10. 7.5 × 8.635   14. 24 ÷ 2.2

   11. .429 × .06   15. .365 ÷ .02

   12. 74.62 × .13   16. 36.98 ÷ 74.6

Fractions

Add: Subtract:

   17. $\frac{1}{2} + \frac{1}{4} + \frac{1}{8}$ 21. $\frac{3}{8} - \frac{1}{5}$

   18. $\frac{2}{3} + \frac{3}{4}$ 22. $\frac{16}{23} - \frac{11}{13}$

   19. $\frac{6}{7} + \frac{5}{8} + \frac{19}{21}$ 23. $\frac{1}{5} - \frac{1}{8}$

   20. $\frac{4}{5} + \frac{2}{9}$ 24. $\frac{2}{3} - \frac{8}{9}$

Multiply: Divide:

   25. $\frac{2}{3} \times \frac{4}{7}$ 29. $\frac{1}{2} \div \frac{1}{3}$

   26. $\frac{4}{5} \times \frac{1}{3}$ 30. $\frac{3}{4} \div \frac{1}{2}$

   27. $\frac{7}{10} \times \frac{1}{2} \times \frac{2}{3}$ 31. $\frac{12}{19} \div \frac{6}{7}$

   28. $\frac{3}{4} \times \frac{1}{3} \times \frac{3}{8}$ 32. $25 \div \frac{1}{2}$

Negative Numbers

Add:

   33. (-2) + (3)

   34. (-28) + (-12)

   35. (-16) + (-3) + (-15) + (-21)

36. (-8) + (-5) + (35)

Subtract:

37. (-8) - (-5)
38. (16) - (-12)
39. (-23) - (-21)
40. (263) - (-158)

Multiply: Divide:

41. (-5) × (-2)   45. (-4) ÷ (-2)
42. (4) × (-6)   46. (8) ÷ (-3)
43. (-10) × (-14)   47. (-26) ÷ (12)
44. (-21) × (7)   48. (-15) ÷ (-21)

Percents and Proportions

49. A class is made up of 12 males and 15 females. What proportion is female?

50. The same class has 10 black students and 17 white students. What percent is black?

51. If 22% of the students in the class are black females, how many are there?

52. How many black males are in the class?

Absolute Value	± Problems	Exponents
53. 6 + |-5|	57. 10 ± 18	61. 6^2
54. |7| + (-3)	58. 52 ± 6.5	62. 2.38^2
55. |-8| - |-6|	59. -8 ± 3.25	63. 18.5^2
56. 10 × |-4|	60. .32 ± .35	64. $.009^2$

COMPLEX PROBLEMS (Round all answers to three decimal places.)

65. $\dfrac{8 + 1 + 4 + 6}{3}$

66. $\dfrac{(10 - 6 - 5 + 2)^2 + (6 - 3 - 4 + 4)^2}{4(5 + 3)}$

67. $$\dfrac{(66 - \frac{12^2}{10}) + (75 - \frac{8^2}{5})}{10 - 1}$$

68. $$\dfrac{(5)(20) - (15)(6)}{\sqrt{[(5)(38) - (150)][(5)(22) - (93)]}}$$

69. $$\dfrac{\frac{225}{9} - (12)(6)}{(8.5)(6.3)}$$

70. $$36 - (1.96)\left(\frac{2}{\sqrt{100}}\right)$$

71. $$\dfrac{5.6 - 12.4}{\sqrt{\left(\frac{32 + 41}{5 + 6 - 2}\right)\left(\frac{1}{6} + \frac{1}{3}\right)}}$$

72. $$\sqrt{\dfrac{21 - \frac{(-8)^2}{6}}{6}}$$

73. $$\sqrt{\dfrac{\left[68 - \frac{(5)^2}{2} + 54 - \frac{(11)^2}{5}\right]}{6(8 - 1)}}$$

74. $$\dfrac{\left(\frac{112}{8} - \frac{73 + 84}{8 + 8}\right)2}{\frac{13.26}{8} + \frac{13.26}{8 + 8}}$$

Simple Algebra (Solve for x.)

75. $\dfrac{x + 5}{3} = 4.25$

76. $\dfrac{24 - 8}{x} = 6.42$

77. $\dfrac{15 - 7}{4} = 2x - 2$

78. $\dfrac{12 - 3}{3} = \dfrac{3x + 5}{2}$

ANSWERS TO PROBLEMS

CHAPTER 1

Multiple-Choice Questions

1.	2	5.	4	9.	3	13.	4
2.	3	6.	2	10.	2	14.	1
3.	4	7.	3	11.	3		
4.	1	8.	4	12.	3		

Short-Answer Questions

1. A descriptive statistic is an index number that is in some way characteristic of or informative about a large group of numbers. Inferential statistics is a method of drawing conclusions about populations from samples taken from populations.

2. A population is a set of measurements on all the members of a group. A sample is a set of measurements on some part of that group.

3. Different numbers on an <u>interval scale</u> have the following relationships: different numbers stand for different things (or amounts); larger numbers mean more of the thing than smaller numbers; and the differences between numbers on the scale are all the same. <u>Ordinal scales</u> have only the first and second characteristics named here.

Problems

1A. a. Brand of paper towel
      b. Amount of punch drained off
      c. Time for absorption, kind of liquid
          absorbed, weight of rolls equal
      d. All SOPPO paper towels (or all SLURPY
          or GRUNGE GATHERER)
      e. One roll of paper towels of a certain
          brand
      f. The measurements of the amount of
          liquid drained off for each brand are
          statistics.
      g. The mean amount of liquid drained off
          all rolls of paper towels of a partic-
          ular brand.
      h. Brand of towel
      i. Amount of liquid drained off and time
          are measured on a ratio scale.
      j. This study of paper towels, based on
          only one observation of SOPPO, SLURPY,
          and GRUNGE GATHERER, claimed to show
          that SOPPO absorbed more raspberry
          punch than the other two towels.

1B. a. Classification of patient (depressed
          or manic)
      b. Amount of biogenic amine neurotrans-
          mitter in brain
      c. Time in hospital
      d. Hospitalized manics (or hospitalized
          depressives)
      e. Either of the two groups studied
      f. Mean amount of neurotransmitters in
          one of the groups
      g. Mean amount of neurotransmitters in a
          population of patients
      h. Diagnosis
      i. Time in hospital--ratio; amount of
          neurotransmitter--probably ratio
      j. Recently hospitalized depressives have
          low levels of biogenic amine neuro-
          transmitters and manics have high
          levels.

1C.   a.   Size of brainstorming group (one or five)
      b.   Number of solutions generated
      c.   Time allowed to generate solutions, groups equated by random assignment
      d.   All high school students who might brainstorm a problem on an individual (or group) basis
      e.   Subjects in this study who brain-stormed a problem on an individual (or group) basis
      f.   Mean number of solutions generated by individuals (or groups)
      g.   Mean number of solutions that all high school students will generate on an individual (or group) basis
      h.   Problem-solving techniques
      i.   Number of solutions generated--ratio scale
      j.   Individuals working alone create more brainstorming solutions than individuals working in groups of five.

1D.   a.   Anxiety (high and low)
      b.   Number of errors
      c.   All subjects had normal vision, all were introductory psychology students
      d.   All high- (or low-) anxiety college students
      e.   The 21 high- (or low-) anxiety college students
      f.   Mean number of errors made by the 21 high- (or low-) anxiety subjects
      g.   Mean number of errors which would be made by all high- (or low-) anxiety college students
      h.   Position of the gap
      i.   Number of errors--ratio scale, anxiety--ordinal to interval scale
      j.   High-anxiety individuals have a stronger drive for closure than low-anxiety individuals.

2.   a.   4.25–4.35 minutes
      b.   5.50 to 6.50 errors
      c.   56.745°–56.755°C

129

d. $45.495−45.505
e. 48.5−49.5 grams

3. a. 5   b. 6.4   c. .82   d. 1
    e. 652.4

4. a. I   b. D   c. I   d. I

5. a. I   b. D   c. D   d. I

6. a. quantitative, 413.5 to 414.5
    b. quantitative, 15.5 to 16.5
    c. qualitative
    d. quantitative, 2.95 to 3.05
    e. quantitative, 101.85 to 101.95
    f. quantitative, 23.945 to 23.955

7. a. sonnets: qualitative
    b. paper: 2.5 to 3.5
    c. protozoans: qualitative
    d. time: 4.95 to 5.05
    e. gold: 6.045 to 6.055
    f. decibels: 7.945 to 7.955
    g. IQ: 99.5 to 100.5

8. independent variable--kind of motive
    dependent variable--amount of shock
      tolerated
    extraneous variables--experience in box,
      experience of handlers, others

9. independent variable: experience of early
      psychic trauma
    dependent variable: cancer
    extraneous variables: age of subjects,
      residence of subjects, others.

CHAPTER 2

Multiple-Choice Questions

1. 4   5. 4   9. 3   13. 2
2. 2   6. 4   10. 3   14. 3
3. 4   7. 1   11. 2
4. 1   8. 1   12. 4

130

Short-Answer Questions

1. Severely skewed data, open-ended categories, ordinal data.

2. A frequency polygon consists of dots connected by lines and is used to present one or more sets of quantitative data. A histogram, which consists of touching bars, is used to present one set of quantitative data. A bar graph has space between the bars and is used to present qualitative data.

3. The conclusion is correct only if the number of dollars invested in each of the three divisions is the same--a highly unlikely event.

4. The median would be smaller. The mean is pulled toward the higher scores when a distribution is skewed, as this one is. The median, unaffected by skewness, remains in the center of the distribution.

5.   a.   Bar graph with TV shows on the abscissa. TV shows are values on a nominal variable.
     b.   Histogram or frequency polygon with income on the abscissa. Income is a ratio variable.
     c.   Histogram or ~~frequency~~ polygon with day of the week on the abscissa. Day of the week is interval data. *Line graph*
     d.   Bar graph with events named on the abscissa. Events constitute a nominal variable.
     e.   Line graph with calories on the ordinate and weeks or days on the abscissa. Neither of the two variables is a frequency count.
     f.   Histogram or frequency polygon with hours on the abscissa. Hours are measured on an interval scale in this case. *Line graph*

g. Bar graph with the four pizza places indicated on the abscissa. Pizza places make up a nominal variable.

Problems

1. a. $N = 23$; $\frac{23}{2} = 11.5$. The median is in the interval that has seven frequencies, the interval from 5.5 to 6.5. Working from the bottom of the distribution, there are seven frequencies below 5.5. 4.5 more frequencies are needed $(11.5 - 7 = 4.5)$. $\frac{4.5}{7} = .64$. $5.5 + .64 = 6.14$. The median is 6.14.

 Working from the top, $6.5 - \frac{2.5}{7} = 6.5 - .36 = 6.14$. The median is 6.14.

   b. $N = 48$; $\frac{48}{2} = 24$. The median is in the interval 33–35, which has six frequencies. The interval width, i, is 3. Working from the top of the distribution, there are 23 frequencies above the class limit, 35.5. One more frequency is needed $(24 - 23 = 1)$. $(\frac{1}{6})(3) = 0.5$. $35.5 - 0.5 = 35.0$. The median is 35.0.

 Working from the bottom, $32.5 + (\frac{5}{6})(3) = 32.5 + 2.5 = 35.0$. The median is 35.0.

   c. $N = 29$; $\frac{29}{2} = 14.5$. The median is in the interval 25–29, which has nine frequencies. The interval width, i, is 5. Working from the top of the distribution, there are 14 frequencies above the class limit of 29.5. 0.5 more frequencies are needed $(14.5 - 14 = 0.5)$. $(\frac{0.5}{9})(5) = .28$, $29.5 - .28 = 29.22$. The median is 29.22.

 Working from the bottom, $24.5 + (\frac{8.5}{9})(5) = 24.5 + 4.72 = 29.22$. The median is 29.22.

   d. $N = 47$; $\frac{47}{2} = 23.5$. The median is in the interval 53–57, which has eight frequencies and an interval width (i) of 5. Working from the bottom of the distribution, there are 22 frequencies

below the class limit of 52.5. 1.5
more frequencies are needed (23.5 - 22
= 1.5). $(\frac{1.5}{8})(5)$ = .94. 52.5 + .94 =
53.44. The median is 53.44.
    Working from the top, 57.5 -
$(\frac{6.5}{8})(5)$ = 57.5 - 4.06 = 53.44. The
median is 53.44.

2. These data could be grouped with i = 3 or
    i = 5. We chose to use i = 5 with multi-
    ples of 5 at the midpoints.

Class Interval	f	fX		
123–127	1	125		
118–122	2	240		
113–117	2	230	$\bar{X} = \frac{3075}{31}$	
108–112	2	220		
103–107	4	420	= 99.19	
98–102	7	700		
93–97	4	380		
88–92	4	360		
83–87	1	85		
78–82	3	240		
73–77	1	75		
Σ	31	3075		

Median: $\frac{31}{2}$ = 15.5, so the median is a
point which will have 15.5 scores above and
below it. There are 13 scores between the
93–97 interval and the bottom of the distribution; therefore, the median is some-
place in the 98–102 interval. That
interval contains seven scores. Only 2.5
of those are needed (15.5 - 13 = 2.5).
Converting $\frac{2.5}{7}$ into a proportion gives you
.3571. Take .3571 of the interval size, 5,
and you have 1.7855 score points to add to
the lower limit of the interval. 97.5
+ 1.7855 = 99.2855 = median.
    The mode is 100--the midpoint of the
interval 98–102, because that interval
contains the greatest number of
frequencies.
    The data constitute a sample taken
from a population of all right-handed

females who might become left-brain damaged.

Either a frequency polygon or a histogram could be used to graph the data.

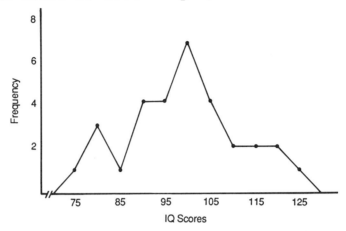

3. These data are measured on a nominal scale; therefore, a simple frequency distribution, a bar graph, and the mode are the appropriate methods and statistic.

X	f
4	6
3	3
2	5
1	3
0	23

The modal response was "auto," which was given by 62 percent of the respondents.

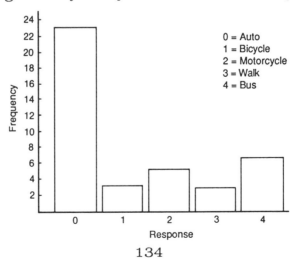

0 = Auto
1 = Bicycle
2 = Motorcycle
3 = Walk
4 = Bus

4. Since the scores range from 0 to 2, and are nominal data, a simple frequency distribution is the only appropriate grouping.

X	f
2	16
1	3
0	1

$\Sigma f = N = 21$

The modal response, looking at his watch a second time, was given by 76 percent of the respondents.

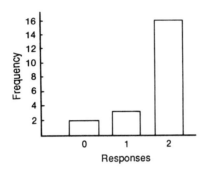

5. A.

Class Interval	X	f	
66–68	67	1	
63–65	64	0	Median = 48.1
60–62	61	3	
57–59	58	4	
54–56	55	1	
51–53	52	3	
48–50	49	5	
45–47	46	0	
42–44	45	6	
39–41	40	5	
36–38	37	2	
33–35	34	1	
30–32	31	1	

B.

Class Interval	X	f	
65−69	67	1	
60−64	62	2	
55−59	57	0	Median = 27.0
50−54	52	2	
45−49	47	4	
40−44	42	2	
35−39	37	4	
30−34	32	0	
25−29	27	5	
20−24	22	2	
15−19	17	6	
10−14	12	2	
5−9	7	1	
0−4	2	4	

Using multiples of 5 at the midpoint:

Class Interval	X	f	
68−72	70	1	
63−67	65	0	
58−62	60	2	
53−57	55	0	
48−52	50	4	Median = 28.3
43−47	45	2	
38−42	40	5	
33−37	35	1	
28−32	30	3	
23−27	25	2	
18−22	20	4	
13−17	15	5	
8−12	10	2	
3−7	5	2	
-2−2	0	2	

CHAPTER 3

Multiple-Choice Questions

1.	2	5.	3	9.	4	13.	3
2.	4	6.	2	10.	3	14.	4
3.	1	7.	2	11.	4	15.	2
4.	4	8.	1	12.	3		

Short-Answer Questions

1. Choose the one store that has the lowest price on apples and buy all three items there. Since milk and cereal have small standard deviations, the price will be about the same at all four stores. The large standard deviation for apples means that prices vary. The cheapest price on apples will represent a much larger savings than the cheapest price on milk.

2. σ is used to describe the variability in a population of data. s is used to estimate the variability in a population of data from the variability of a sample. S is used to describe the variability of a sample of data when you have no intention of drawing inferences about the larger population.

Problems

1.
8-9 Years

X	x	x^2	X^2
28	6	36	784
25	3	9	625
22	0	0	484
19	-3	9	361
16	-6	36	256
Σ = 110	0	90	2510

$\overline{X} = 22$

$S = \sqrt{\dfrac{90}{5}} = 4.24$

$S = \sqrt{\dfrac{2510 - \dfrac{110^2}{5}}{5}} = 4.24$

$z = \dfrac{28 - 22}{4.24} = 1.42$

10–11 Years

X	x	x^2	X^2
32	6	36	1024
30	4	16	900
26	−1	1	625
23	−3	9	529
20	−6	36	400
Σ = 131	0	98	3478

$\overline{X} = 26.2$

$S = \sqrt{\dfrac{98}{5}} = 4.43$

$S = \sqrt{\dfrac{3478 - \dfrac{131^2}{5}}{5}} = 4.43$

$z = \dfrac{32 - 26.2}{4.43} = 1.40$

12–13 Years

X	x	x^2	X^2
51	6	36	2601
49	4	16	2401
45	0	0	2025
42	−3	9	1764
38	−7	49	1444
Σ = 225	0	110	10235

$\overline{X} = 45$

$S = \sqrt{\dfrac{110}{5}} = 4.69$

$S = \sqrt{\dfrac{10235 - \dfrac{225^2}{5}}{5}} = 4.69$

$z = \dfrac{51 - 45}{4.69} = 1.28$

The overall winner is Joe, who had the largest z score.

2. s is appropriate here. The intention of the student in nursing is to find out about neonates in general.

X	f	fX	fX^2
20	3	60	1200
19	4	76	1444
18	10	180	3240
17	5	85	1445
16	2	32	512
15	1	15	225
Σ = 25		448	8066

$$\bar{X} = \frac{448}{25} = 17.92 \qquad s = \sqrt{\frac{8066 - \frac{448^2}{25}}{24}}$$

$$= \sqrt{\frac{37.84}{24}} = 1.26$$

3.

Ina's Class		Dr. Phitt's Class	
X	X^2	X	X^2
82	6724	97	9409
79	6241	96	9216
76	5776	95	9025
75	5625	88	7744
73	5329	87	7569
70	4900	82	6724
68	4624	80	6400
67	4489	79	6241
64	4096	77	5929
62	3844	75	5625
61	3721		
60	3600		
57	3249		
52	2704		
51	2601		
Σ = 997	67,523	Σ = 856	73,882
$\bar{X}$ = 66.47		$\bar{X}$ = 85.60	

$$S = \sqrt{\frac{67,523 - \frac{997^2}{15}}{15}} = 9.15$$

139

$$S = \sqrt{\frac{73,882 - \frac{856^2}{10}}{10}} = 7.80$$

$$z = \frac{60 - 66.47}{9.15} \qquad z = \frac{80 - 85.60}{7.80}$$

$$= -.71 \qquad\qquad = -.72$$

Since Dr. Phitt's score is -.72 and Ina's is -.71, he must concede that his score, relative to his class, was infinitesimally lower than her score relative to her class. The difference, however, was certainly not enough to throw a phitt about!

4.

X	X^2
22	484
19	361
17	289
16	256
15	225
15	225
14	196
14	196
13	169
12	144
12	144
11	121
10	100
9	81
8	64
$\Sigma = 207$	3055

$$\bar{X} = \frac{207}{15} = 13.80$$

$$\Sigma X = 207$$

$$\Sigma X^2 = 3055$$

$$s = \sqrt{\frac{3055 - \frac{207^2}{15}}{14}}$$

$$= 3.76$$

$$s^2 = 14.17$$

5.

X	X^2
45	2025
41	1681
38	1444
35	1225
34	1156
32	1024
29	841
28	784
27	729
25	625

$$\bar{X} = 28.20$$

$$\Sigma X = 423$$

$$\Sigma X^2 = 13,209$$

$$s = \sqrt{\frac{13,209 - \frac{423^2}{15}}{14}}$$

$$= 9.56$$

24	576	$s^2 = 91.46$	
21	441		
17	289		
15	225		
12	144		
$\Sigma = 423$	13,209		

The vigilance task seems to have a more detrimental effect on some people than others, causing variability to increase.

6.

Class Interval	f	X	fX	x	x^2
24–26	5	25	125	9.96	99.2016
21–23	9	22	198	6.96	48.4416
18–20	43	19	817	3.96	15.6816
15–17	53	16	848	.96	.9216
12–14	48	13	624	-2.04	4.1616
9–11	34	10	340	-5.04	25.4016
6–8	8	7	56	-8.04	64.6416
	$\Sigma = 200$		3008		

Class Interval	fx^2	fX^2
24–26	496.0080	3125
21–23	435.9744	4356
18–20	674.3088	15523
15–17	48.8448	13568
12–14	199.7568	8112
9–11	863.6544	3400
6–8	517.1328	392
	$\Sigma = 3235.68$	48476

$$\bar{X} = \frac{3008}{200} = 15.04 \qquad \text{or:}$$

$$s = \sqrt{\frac{3235.68}{199}} \qquad s = \sqrt{\frac{48476 - \frac{3008^2}{200}}{199}}$$

$$= \sqrt{16.2597} \qquad = \sqrt{16.2597}$$

$$= 4.0323 \qquad = 4.0323$$

141

The average age of walking without support is 15 months; however, there is large variability around this average. Children vary from about 7 to 25 months in age for this activity with a standard deviation of 4 months.

CHAPTER 4

Multiple-Choice Questions

1. 4	5. 4	9. 1	13. 3
2. 1	6. 3	10. 4	14. 2
3. 4	7. 1	11. 1	15. 2
4. 2	8. 4	12. 2	

Short-Answer Questions

1. The more self-confidence a recruit has, the less likely he or she will be successful.

2. The regression procedure is a method of fitting a straight line to a bivariate distribution. It can be used to predict scores on one variable given scores on the other variable. It can be used only with quantitative data which are linearly related. The degree of confidence you have in your prediction is directly related to the size of the absolute value of r.

3. a. Nuns and sex offenders are in very close agreement in their rating of the social desirability of responses. Those rated as high by one group are also rated high by the other. Those rated low by one group are rated low by the other.
    b. $b = (.95)(\frac{1.46}{1.32}) = 1.0508$
        $a = 5.59 - (1.0508)(5.86) = -.5677$
        $Y' = -.5677 + (1.0508)(4.30) = 3.95$

        or
        $Y' = (.95)(\frac{1.46}{1.32})(4.30 - 5.86) + 5.59$
        $= 3.95$

4. There is some tendency for students sco~~~g higher on the LSAT to make better grades in the first year of law school than students with relatively low LSAT scores. This tendency, however, is very weak. The LSAT accounts for only about 13% of the variance in grades ($r^2 = .13$) with the other 87% unaccounted for.

    Part of the reason for this low correlation is probably due to truncation of range. In these data the correlation is computed on only those students selected for law school, nearly all of whom had high scores on the LSAT. The range of scores (variability in the scores) is thus restricted. In like manner, grade distributions tend to be restricted to higher grades (mostly A and B). Such restrictions on variability always reduce the size of r.

5. The improvement of the mean from 15 to 21 is the statistic most related to the issue of the effect of the college. The moderate correlation coefficient of .60 shows that those who scored high or low as entering freshmen tend to score high or low, respectively, as juniors.

Problems

1.

Sub-ject	Distance Judgments X	Value Judgments Y	X^2	Y^2	XY
1	8	1	64	1	8
2	4	2	16	4	8
3	7	0	49	0	0
4	9	3	81	9	27
5	3	1	9	1	3
6	0	2	0	4	0
7	4	0	16	0	0
Sum:	35	9	235	19	46

$$\bar{X} = \frac{35}{7} = 5.00 \qquad \bar{Y} = \frac{9}{7} = 1.286$$

$$S_x = \sqrt{\frac{235 - \frac{35^2}{7}}{7}} \qquad S_y = \sqrt{\frac{19 - \frac{9^2}{7}}{7}}$$

$$= 2.928 \qquad\qquad = 1.030$$

$$r = \frac{\frac{46}{7} - (5.00)(1.286)}{(2.928)(1.030)} = .047$$

$$r = \frac{(7)(46) - (35)(9)}{\sqrt{\left[(7)(235) - 35^2\right]\left[(7)(19) - 9^2\right]}}$$

$$= \frac{7}{147.784} = .047$$

The correlation coefficient of .047 shows that a person's degree of conformity when pressured to change a distance judgment is unrelated to that person's conformity when pressured to change a value judgment. In more general terms, there is no relationship between conformity in an objective situation and that in a value situation.

$$b = (.047)\frac{1.030}{2.928} = .017$$

$$a = 1.286 - (.017)(5.00) = 1.203$$

2.

Subject	% Junk Food X	% Body Fat Y	X^2	Y^2	XY
1	46	40	2116	1600	1840
2	32	43	1024	1849	1376
3	29	28	841	784	812
4	23	31	529	961	713
5	20	36	400	1296	720
6	17	25	289	625	425
7	15	20	225	400	300
8	12	12	144	144	144
9	11	15	121	225	165
10	8	19	64	361	152
$\Sigma =$	213	269	5753	8245	6647

a. $\bar{X} = \frac{213}{10} = 21.30$ $\bar{Y} = \frac{269}{10} = 26.90$

$$S_x = \sqrt{\frac{5753 - \frac{213^2}{10}}{10}}   \qquad S_y = \sqrt{\frac{8245 - \frac{269^2}{10}}{10}}$$

$$= 11.0277 \qquad\qquad = 10.0444$$

$$r = \frac{\frac{6649}{10} - (21.30)(26.90)}{(11.0277)(10.0444)} = \frac{91.93}{110.7666}$$

$$= .8299$$

$$r = \frac{(10)(6647) - (213)(269)}{\sqrt{\left[(10)(5753) - (213)^2\right]\left[(10)(8245) - (269)^2\right]}}$$

$$= \frac{9173}{\sqrt{(12161)(10089)}} = \frac{9173}{\sqrt{122692329}}$$

$$= \frac{9173}{11076.6569} = .8281$$

b.

$$b = (.83)\frac{10.0444}{11.0277} = .7560$$

$$a = 26.90 - (.7560)(21.30) = 10.80$$

c. $Y' = 10.80 + (.7560)(25)$
    $= 29.7\%$ body fat

d. No such statement can be made on the
    basis of the data available here.
    Though it would be reasonable to expect
    junk food to make children fat, corre-
    lational data cannot establish it.
    This correlation tells us that the more
    junk food kids eat, the greater their
    percent body fat. It may be that those

who eat more junk food also eat other fattening foods and exercise less.

3.

Subject	X	Y	X^2	Y^2	XY
1	60	28	3600	784	1680
2	57	32	3249	1024	1824
3	52	24	2704	576	1248
4	46	16	2116	256	736
5	41	21	1681	441	861
6	38	14	1444	196	532
7	32	18	1024	324	576
8	29	11	841	121	319
9	25	9	625	81	225
10	19	12	361	144	228
Σ =	399	185	17,645	3947	8229

$$\bar{X} = \frac{399}{10} = 39.9 \qquad \bar{Y} = \frac{185}{10} = 18.5$$

$$S_x = \frac{17,645 - \frac{399^2}{10}}{10} \qquad S_y = \frac{3947 - \frac{185^2}{10}}{10}$$

$$= 13.1335 \qquad\qquad = 7.2422$$

$$r = \frac{\frac{8229}{10} - (39.9)(18.5)}{(13.1335)(7.2422)} = \frac{84.75}{95.1154} = .89$$

$$r = \frac{(10)(8229) - (399)(185)}{\sqrt{\left[(10)(17,645) - (399^2)\right]\left[(10)(3947) - (185^2)\right]}}$$

$$= \frac{8475}{\sqrt{(17,249)(5245)}} = \frac{8475}{9511.6247} = .89$$

There is a strong positive relationship between the two abilities. As the ability to make semantic transformations increases, the ability to make puns also increases. Since $r^2 = .79$, you can conclude that these two abilities are primarily due to some common factor.

4.

Subject	X	Y	X^2	Y^2	XY
1	45	21	2025	441	945
2	42	26	1764	676	1092
3	35	24	1225	576	840
4	31	18	961	324	558
5	26	20	676	400	520
6	22	19	484	361	418
7	17	15	289	225	255
8	12	17	144	289	204
9	10	12	100	144	120
10	8	16	64	256	128
11	5	11	25	121	55
12	1	6	1	36	6
Σ =	254	205	7758	3849	5141

$$\bar{X} = \frac{254}{12} = 21.1667 \qquad \bar{Y} = \frac{205}{12} = 17.0833$$

$$S_x = \sqrt{\frac{7758 - \frac{254^2}{12}}{12}} \qquad S_y = \sqrt{\frac{3849 - \frac{205^2}{12}}{12}}$$

$$= 14.0880 \qquad\qquad = 5.3768$$

$$r = \frac{\frac{5141}{12} - (21.1667)(17.0833)}{(14.0880)(5.3768)} = \frac{66.8196}{75.7484} = .88$$

$$r = \frac{12(5141) - (254)(205)}{\sqrt{\left[(12)(7758) - (254)^2\right]\left[(12)(3849) - (205)^2\right]}}$$

$$= \frac{9622}{\sqrt{(28,580)(4163)}} = \frac{9622}{10,907.7285} = .88$$

Children who read more do tend to have better vocabularies; however, to say that reading improves vocabulary is to make a cause and effect inference. This is not justified on the basis of correlational analysis. Other conclusions are possible. Perhaps children with better vocabularies enjoy reading more. Perhaps children from homes where larger vocabularies are used are also homes where reading is encouraged.

147

CHAPTER 5

Multiple-Choice Questions

1. 3	5. 3	9. 4	13. 3
2. 1	6. 2	10. 4	14. 3
3. 4	7. 4	11. 1	
4. 4	8. 3	12. 2	

Short-Answer Questions

1.   A theoretical distribution is based on mathematics and logic, whereas an empirical distribution is obtained from observations.

2.   The normal curve is a bell-shaped symmetrical distribution. The mean, median, and mode are all the same number. The points of inflection in the curve are at plus and minus one standard deviation and the curve is asymptotic to the X-axis.

3.   The mean will be one inch less, 35 inches, and the standard deviation will be the same, 2 inches.

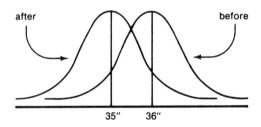

Problems

1.   a. empirical   d. empirical
     b. empirical   e. empirical
     c. empirical   f. empirical

2.   a. The easiest way to work these problems is to convert all measurements to inches.

$$z = \frac{48 - 51}{2} = -1.50,$$

proportion = .5000 + .4332 = .9332

b. $z = \frac{50 - 51}{2} = -.50,\ p = .3085$

$z = \frac{54 - 51}{2} = 1.50,\ p = .0668$

.3085 + .0668 = .3753, the proportion who are left out

c. $\frac{15}{80} = .19$, the probability of choosing one from the subgroup led by Cephu.

3. a. $z = \frac{23 - 20}{4} = .75,\ p = .2266$

b. $z = \frac{27 - 20}{4} = 1.75,\ p = .0401$

c. $z = \frac{36 - 20}{4} = 4.00,\ p = .00003$

The probability of obtaining 36 matches in 100 attempts by chance alone is .00003. Some other explanation (like ESP or cheating) seems more likely.

d. (.077)(3) = .231

4. a. All measurements must be converted to the same scale. For our answers we used pounds.

$z = 2.81$

$2.81 = \frac{X - 40}{.25}$ Adding the eight ounces lost in transit: 40.7025 + .5 = 41.2025 pounds

.7025 = X - 40

X = 40.7025

b. (.0025)(5,000,000) = 12,500 boxes

5. a. $z = \frac{1 - 7}{3.74} = -1.60$, proportion $= .0548$

    b. Figure 6.1 shows a proportion of .077

    c. The distribution of playing cards is rectangular but the normal curve was used to calculate the proportion .0548.

    d. $\frac{12}{52} = .23$

6. $z = \frac{175.5 - 177.4}{6.1} = -.31$

    proportion $= .5000 + .1217 = .6217$

7. a. $z = \frac{7 - 6.9}{.34} = .29$, proportion $= .3859$

    b. $z = \frac{6 - 6.9}{.34} = -2.65$, proportion $= .004$

    c. $z = \frac{6.5 - 6.9}{.34} = 1.18$,

    proportion $= .3810$

    $z = \frac{7.2 - 6.9}{.34} = .88$, proportion $= .3106$

    $.3810 + .3106 = .6916$

    d. $z = \frac{7.5 - 6.9}{.34} = 1.76$,

    proportion $= .0392$.

    $(.0392)(3000) = 117.6 = 118$

    e. $1.28 = \frac{x - 6.9}{.34}$

    $.4353 = x - 6.9$

    $x = 7.34$

CHAPTER 6

Multiple-Choice Questions

1.	2	5.	2	9.	3	13.	2
2.	3	6.	3	10.	4	14.	1
3.	2	7.	3	11.	1	15.	4
4.	2	8.	2	12.	4		

Short-Answer Questions

1. The Central Limit Theorem says that the form of the sampling distribution of the mean of any population will have a mean equal to μ, a standard deviation equal to $\frac{\sigma}{\sqrt{N}}$, and will approach a normal curve if sample size is large.

2. a. Draw many, many random samples with N = 50 from the population. Find the range for each sample. Arrange all these ranges into a frequency distribution.

   b. No. The mean of the sampling distribution of the range will always be less than the population range. Using the words of mathematical statisticians, the sample range is a biased estimator of the population range.

3. A sampling distribution can be found for any statistic. The sampling distribution of the mean is one example.

Problems

1. According to the Central Limit Theorem, the sampling distribution of the mean will be normal, regardless of the shape of the population distribution, if the sample size is 30 or greater. The techniques of Chapter 6 are, therefore, appropriate for this skewed distribution when the sample size is this large.

2. $\bar{X} = \frac{\Sigma X}{N} = \frac{3616}{49} = 73.80$

$$s = \sqrt{\frac{\Sigma X^2 - \frac{(\Sigma X)^2}{N}}{N-1}} = \sqrt{\frac{271456 - \frac{(3616)^2}{49}}{48}}$$

$$= 9.80$$

$$s_{\overline{X}} = \frac{s}{\sqrt{N}} = \frac{9.80}{\sqrt{49}} = 1.40$$

$$z = \frac{\overline{X} - \mu}{s_{\overline{X}}} = \frac{73.80 - 75.40}{1.40} = -1.14$$

$$p = .1271$$

Almost 13 times in 100 you would expect by chance alone to get a sample of 49 with a mean of 73.8 from a population with a mean of 75.4. The evidence is not at all strong that male vegetarians weigh less than the national average.

For comparison purposes, the mean weight of average-height (5'4") 18- to 24-year-old females is 134 pounds.

3. a. $\overline{X} = \frac{2217}{30} = 73.90$

$$s = \sqrt{\frac{163,841.40 - \frac{2217^2}{30}}{29}} = 0.4194$$

$$s_{\overline{X}} = \frac{0.4194}{\sqrt{30}} = 0.0766$$

LL = 73.90 - 1.96(.0766) = 73.75
UL = 73.90 + 1.96(.0766) = 74.05

b. $\overline{X} = \frac{2223}{30} = 74.10$

The mean of this sample of 30 (74.1) is out of the range of the confidence interval. The manufacturing process needs to be adjusted so that the tubes will be shorter.

4. Each person's sample is likely to be different. What is important is the procedure.
    a. Identify each score with a one-digit number from 0 to 9.
    b. Haphazardly find a place to start in the table of random numbers.

c. Record the first six digits you come to, ignoring a digit that appears more than once.

d. Translate the six digits into the six scores, which now constitute a random sample.

5. $s_{\overline{X}} = \frac{100}{\sqrt{50}} = 14.14$

$z = \frac{\overline{X} - \mu}{s_{\overline{X}}} = \frac{725 - 750}{14.14} = -1.77$

$p = .0384$

The claim is on somewhat shaky ground. If the claim of 750 hours is correct, you would expect to get a mean of 725 or lower from 50 bulbs less than 4% of the time.

6. $\overline{X} = \frac{\Sigma X}{N} = \frac{1275}{75} = 17.00$

$s = \sqrt{\frac{\Sigma X^2 - \frac{(\Sigma X)^2}{N}}{N-1}} = \sqrt{\frac{23525 - \frac{(1275)^2}{75}}{74}} = 5.00$

$s_{\overline{X}} = \frac{5}{\sqrt{75}} = .58$

$LL = \overline{X} - z(s_{\overline{X}}) = 17.00 - 2.58(.58) = 15.50$
$UL = \overline{X} + z(s_{\overline{X}}) = 17.00 + 2.58(.58) = 18.50$

The teacher can be 99 percent confident that in her state the mean mathematics ability on the test is between 15.50 and 18.50.

CHAPTER 7

Multiple-Choice Questions

1.	1	5.	3	9.	3	13.	1
2.	4	6.	4	10.	3	14.	1
3.	3	7.	2	11.	4	15.	3
4.	2	8.	2	12.	2	16.	2

Short-Answer Questions

1. a. Actual difference between the populations. The greater the actual difference, the more likely the rejection of the null hypothesis.
   b. The size of the standard error of a difference. The smaller it is, the more likely the rejection of the null hypothesis. It can be made smaller by increasing sample size or reducing sample variability.
   c. Alpha. The larger alpha is, the more likely the rejection of the null hypothesis.

2. The probability is .01 of obtaining a difference as large as the one observed if there is really no difference between the two populations.

3. For $z = 1.05$, $p > .05$. Since this is a test of Rosenthal's theory, the only result of interest is $\mu_{favorable} > \mu_{unfavorable}$--a one-tailed test. A probability $> .05$ does not support such a hypothesis. There is no significant difference between the means.

4. For $z = 3.19$, $p < .01$. The group receiving wine with dinner expressed greater self-confidence than those not receiving wine.

Problems

1. This is the same answer we used for the textbook problem. Regardless of the material you choose to include, your essay should have good introductory and concluding paragraphs. As for content, the purpose of inferential statistics should receive prominent attention along with the logic of inferential statistics. Sampling should be covered. Your essay should explain the null hypothesis and the alternative hypothesis and describe sampling

distributions as the method to determine the probability of obtaining the observed results <u>if the null hypothesis is true.</u> Level of significance and possible deci-sions about the population should be included.

2. If you worked the problems yourself, you probably were stumped for a while on No. 8. The method (set) you had developed by solv-ing the first seven did not work for the eighth. How adaptable were you? Did you abandon your set quickly when it did not work, or did you stick with it? To com-plete the data analysis:

$$s_{set} = \sqrt{\frac{\Sigma X^2 - \frac{\Sigma X^2}{N}}{N-1}} = 2.00; \quad s_{\overline{X}} = \frac{2}{\sqrt{49}} = .2857$$

$$s_{no\ set} = \sqrt{\frac{\Sigma X^2 - \frac{\Sigma X^2}{N}}{N-1}} = 6.00;$$

$$s_{\overline{X}} = \frac{6}{\sqrt{49}} = .8571$$

$$s_{\overline{X}_1 - \overline{X}_2} = \sqrt{s_{\overline{X}_1}^2 + s_{\overline{X}_2}^2} = .9035$$

$$z = \frac{\overline{X}_1 - \overline{X}_2}{s_{\overline{X}_1 - \overline{X}_2}} = \frac{16 - 4}{.9035} = 13.28$$

Such large z scores are not found in Table C in your text, but the meaning is quite clear--a very small probability. Thus, conclude that set was detrimental to seeing the simple solution of "fill the 28, and then pour off enough to fill the 3, leaving 25."

3. The phenomenon illustrated here is called reminiscence--an improvement in performance due to rest. It is often found in motor skills tasks. William James described the phenomenon of improvement without practice

when he said that we learn to swim in the winter and to ice skate in the summer. For these data:

$$s_0 = \sqrt{\frac{\Sigma X^2 - \frac{(\Sigma X)^2}{N}}{N-1}} = .8764 \qquad s_6 = .9330$$

$$z = \frac{\overline{X}_1 - \overline{X}_2}{s_{\overline{X}_1} - s_{\overline{X}_2}} = \frac{1.2 - 0.8}{\sqrt{\left(\frac{.8764}{\sqrt{64}}\right)^2 + \left(\frac{.9330}{\sqrt{64}}\right)^2}} = \frac{.4}{.16}$$

$$= 2.50$$

$p < .05$

Conclude that performance on the pursuit rotor is better after a six-month rest than it is immediately after learning.

4. $$z = \frac{1.2 - .8}{\sqrt{\left(\frac{2}{\sqrt{62}}\right)^2 + \left(\frac{2}{\sqrt{64}}\right)^2}} = \frac{.4}{.354} = 1.13,$$

$p > .05$

Retain the null hypothesis. Note that the difference between means of this problem and that of the reminiscence problem is the same--.4. In this problem, the difference was not significant due to the larger standard deviations. Both the size of the mean difference and the variability about the means are important.

5. $$s_{\text{Indian}} = \sqrt{\frac{\Sigma X^2 - \frac{(\Sigma X)^2}{N}}{N-1}} = 3.00$$

$s_{\text{Anglo}} = 3.00$

$$z = \frac{15.0 - 14.9}{\sqrt{\left(\frac{3}{\sqrt{144}}\right)^2 + \left(\frac{3}{\sqrt{144}}\right)^2}} = \frac{.1}{.35} = .28$$

$p > .05$

The age at which Indian and Anglo children walk is not significantly different. Or in terms of the broader question, beginning to walk does not appear to be dependent on lots of practice.

CHAPTER 8

Multiple-Choice Questions

1. 1	5. 4	9. 2	13. 4
2. 1	6. 1	10. 1	14. 4
3. 2	7. 4	11. 4	15. 3
4. 3	8. 2	12. 3	

Short-Answer Questions

1. In a correlated-samples design, there is a logical reason to pair each score in one group with a score in the other group. In an independent-samples design, there is no logical reason for such pairing.

2. a. Correlated samples; df = 13
   b. Correlated samples; df = 20
   c. Independent samples; df = 28
   d. Independent samples; df = 22
   e. Correlated samples; df = 33

3. There are two ways you could have worked this problem: a t test or Table A. The t test answer is as follows:

$$t = (r) \sqrt{\frac{N - 2}{1 - r^2}} = (.40) \sqrt{\frac{173}{.84}} = 5.74$$

$$t_{.001} (120) = 3.373$$

From Table A you can see that an r = .3211 has a probability of .001 with 100 df. An r = .40 with 174 df, then, will have an even lower probability. It is very unlikely that the correlation of .40 came from a population with a correlation of

157

.00. There is some relationship between SAT scores and first semester freshman grades.

Problems

1.

Subject	Before	After	D	D^2
1	5	6	-1	1
2	4	4	0	0
3	3	5	-2	4
4	3	4	-1	1
5	2	4	-2	4
6	2	3	-1	1
7	1	3	-2	4
8	0	2	-2	4

$$\Sigma = 20 \quad 31 \quad -11 \quad 19$$

$$\overline{X} = 2.50 \quad 3.8750$$

$$s_D = \sqrt{\frac{19 - \frac{(-11)^2}{8}}{7}} = \sqrt{\frac{19 - 15.1250}{7}}$$

$$= \sqrt{\frac{3.8750}{7}} = \sqrt{.5536} = .7440$$

$$s_{\overline{D}} = \frac{.7440}{\sqrt{8}} = \frac{.7440}{2.8284} = .2630$$

$$t = \frac{2.50 - 3.8750}{.2630} = \frac{-1.3750}{.2630} = 5.2281;$$

$$p < .01$$

$$df = N - 1 = 8 - 1 = 7 \qquad t_{.01} (7) = 3.499$$

The boys displayed more hostility toward the minority groups after frustration than before, even though the minority groups were in no way responsible for their frustration.

2.

	Detached	Involved
ΣX =	114	140
ΣX^2 =	1996	3432

158

$$\bar{X} = 16.2857 \quad\quad 23.3333$$

$$t = \frac{16.2857 - 23.3333}{\sqrt{\left(\dfrac{1996 - \dfrac{114^2}{7} + 3432 - \dfrac{140^2}{6}}{7 + 6 + 2}\right)\left(\dfrac{1}{7} + \dfrac{1}{6}\right)}}$$

$$= \frac{-7.0476}{\sqrt{\left(\dfrac{139.4286 + 165.3333}{11}\right)(.1429 + .1667)}}$$

$$= \frac{-7.0476}{\sqrt{8.5777}} = \frac{-7.0476}{2.9288} = 2.4063; \quad\quad p < .01$$

$$t_{.01}\,(11) = 2.201.$$

Since the calculated t for this problem is larger than the tabled value, the null hypothesis is rejected. Heart rate increased more in the group instructed to become involved in the movie. Apparently, those instructed to remain detached were more able to control their emotions than those instructed to become involved.

3. Litter Number	No Experimental Neurosis	Experimental Neurosis	D	D^2
1	63	88	-25	625
2	59	90	-31	961
3	52	74	-22	484
4	51	78	-27	729
5	46	78	-32	1024
6	44	61	-17	289
7	38	54	-16	256
$\Sigma =$	353	523	-170	4368
$\bar{X} =$	50.4286	74.7143		

$$s_D = \frac{4368 - \dfrac{(-170)^2}{7}}{6} = 6.3170$$

$$s_{\bar{D}} = \frac{6.3170}{\sqrt{7}} = 2.3876$$

$$t_{.05}\,(6) = 2.447$$

159

LL = (50.4286 - 74.7143) - (2.447)(2.3876)
   = 18.4432
UL = (50.4286 - 74.7143) + (2.447)(2.3876)
   = 30.1282

Since zero is not contained in the confidence interval, the null hypothesis of no difference between means is rejected. More of the alcoholic milk was consumed by cats subjected to an experimental neurosis. We are 95% confident that the population difference is between 18.44 and 30.13 cubic centimeters.

4.

	Shown	Not Shown
ΣX	80	118
ΣX^2	1120	2392
$\overline{X}$	13.3333	19.6667
s	3.2660	3.7771

$$s_{\overline{X}_1} = \frac{3.2660}{\sqrt{6}} = 1.3333 \qquad s_{\overline{X}_2} = \frac{3.7771}{\sqrt{6}} = 1.5420$$

$$s_{\overline{X}_1 - \overline{X}_2} = \sqrt{1.3333^2 + 1.5420^2}$$

$$= \sqrt{1.7777 + 2.3778} = 2.0385$$

$$t = \frac{13.3333 - 19.6667}{2.0385} = \frac{-6.3334}{2.0385} = -3.1069$$

or

$$t = \frac{13.3333 - 19.6667}{\sqrt{\dfrac{1120 - \dfrac{(80)^2}{6} + 2392 + \dfrac{(118)^2}{6}}{(6)(5)}}}$$

$$= \frac{-6.3334}{\sqrt{\dfrac{53.3333 + 71.3333}{30}}} = \frac{-6.3334}{\sqrt{4.1556}}$$

$$= \frac{-6.3334}{2.0385} = -3.1069$$

160

$t_{.05}$ (10) = 2.228. Since the obtained t is larger than the tabled t, the difference between means is significant. The animals shown the location of the food found it faster. Hobhouse must have done the study. (He did do a similar one.)

5.

	Success	Failure
ΣX	228	103
ΣX^2	5414	1449
$\overline{X}$	22.80	12.8750

$$s_{\overline{X}_1-\overline{X}_2} = \sqrt{\left(\frac{5414 - \frac{(228)^2}{10} + 1449 - \frac{(103)^2}{8}}{10 + 8 - 2}\right)\left(\frac{1}{10} + \frac{1}{8}\right)}$$

$$= \sqrt{(21.1547)(.225)} = 4.7598 = 2.1817$$

$t_{.01}$ (16) = 2.921

LL = (22.80 - 12.8750) - (2.9210)(2.1817)

    = 9.9250 - 6.3727 = 3.5523

UL = (22.80 - 12.8750) + (2.9210)(2.1817)

    = 9.9250 + 6.3727 = 16.2977

The psychologist can have 99% confidence that the test-score difference between successes and failures is between 3.55 and 16.30 points. Since zero is not within that range, she can conclude that the test does discriminate between applicants who will succeed and those who will fail on the job.

6.

Subject	Before	After	D	D^2
1	44	45	-1	1
2	40	35	4	16
3	39	37	2	4
4	36	33	3	9
5	35	32	3	9
6	34	36	-2	4
7	32	32	0	0
8	28	29	-1	1
9	23	19	4	16

Subject	Before	After	D	D²
10	23	18	5	25
11	19	19	0	0
12	15	14	1	1
Σ =	368	349	18	86
X̄ =	30.6667	29.0833		

$$s_D = \sqrt{\frac{86 - \frac{18^2}{12}}{11}} = \sqrt{\frac{86 - 27}{11}} = \sqrt{\frac{59}{11}} = \sqrt{5.3636}$$

$$= 2.3160$$

$$s_{\bar{D}} = \frac{2.3160}{\sqrt{12}} = \frac{2.3160}{3.4641} = .6686$$

$$t = \frac{30.6667 - 29.0833}{.6686} = \frac{1.58}{.6686} = 2.368$$

$$df = 12 - 1 = 11 \qquad t_{.05}(11) = 2.201$$

Since the calculated t is greater than the t value tabled at the .05 level for 11 df, Dr. Loveless's hypothesis is supported.

CHAPTER 9

Multiple-Choice Questions

1. 4	5. 3	9. 2	13. 3
2. 3	6. 2	10. 1	14. 2
3. 3	7. 3	11. 1	15. 2
4. 2	8. 1	12. 4	

Interpretation

1. The F value produced by the ratio of the two mean squares is 6.04. The tabled F value at the .01 level for 2 and 32 df is 5.34. Thus, there are significant differences among the hospital populations in improvement scores.
   The $s_{\bar{x}}$ value for Tukey tests is 1.31. The tabled value for HSD at the .01 level for three groups and a df_{wg} of 32 is 4.46. When England and Crimea are compared the

HSD value is 4.58. (The value for the France-Crimea comparison is even larger.) A comparison of England and France produces an HSD of 0.76. The conclusion is that patients in the military hospital in Crimea showed significantly higher improvement scores than patients in either English or French hospitals. The English and French hospitals were not significantly different.

2. $F_{.01}$ (2.55) = 5.01. The obtained F (5.75) is significant, p < .01. $HSD_{.01}$ = 4.37. Since the obtained HSD (4.50) is greater than 4.37, conclude that the difference between those experiencing severe embarrassment and mild embarrassment is significantly beyond the .01 level. High scores indicate favorable attitudes, so those who were most embarrassed had a more favorable attitude toward the discussion than those who had experienced only mild embarrassment. Reducing the embarrassment further seemed to have no significant effect, since the difference between the mild- and no-embarrassment groups failed to reach a significant level.

3. The ANOVA method described in Chapter 9 requires independent groups. These data are correlated due to the fact that each wine taster rated all four wines. A repeated-measures design is required for this problem.

Problems

1.

	Very Predictable	Fairly Predictable	Unpre- dictable
	8	16	18
	13	11	19
	11	15	22
	8		16
			15
ΣX	40	42	90
ΣX^2	418	602	1650
$\overline{X}$	10	14	18

$$SS_{tot} = 2670 - \frac{172^2}{12} = 204.67$$

$$SS_{groups} = \frac{40^2}{4} + \frac{42^2}{3} + \frac{90^2}{5} - \frac{172^2}{12} = 142.67$$

$$SS_{wg} = \frac{418 - 40^2}{4} + \frac{602 - 42^2}{3} + \frac{1650 - 90^2}{5}$$

$$= 62.00$$

CHECK: $142.67 + 62.00 = 204.67$

Source	SS	df	MS	F
Between Groups	142.67	2	71.33	10.35
Within Groups	62.00	9	6.89	
Total	204.67	11		

$F_{.01}$ (2,9) = 8.02. The three schedules produced significantly different amounts of
persistence during extinction. Three Tukey
HSD tests produce

HSD (Very vs. Fairly) = 2.84
HSD (Fairly vs. Un) = 2.96
HSD (Very vs. Un) = 6.45

$HSD_{.01}$ = 5.43. The amount of persistence
during extinction depends on the predictability of reinforcement during learning.
Unpredictable reinforcement leads to significantly more persistence than does very
predictable reinforcement.

2.

	WW II	Korean	Viet Nam Hospitalized	Viet Nam Normal
	2	7	9	7
	5	4	7	3
	7	9	12	10
	2	4	12	8
ΣX	16	24	40	28
ΣX^2	82	162	418	222
$\overline{X}$	4	6	10	7

$$SS_{tot} = 884 - \frac{108^2}{16} = 155.00$$

$$SS_{war} = \frac{16^2 + 24^2 + 40^2 + 28^2}{4} - \frac{108^2}{16} = 75.00$$

$$SS_{wg} = \left(82 - \frac{16^2}{4}\right) + \left(162 - \frac{24^2}{4}\right) + \left(418 - \frac{40^2}{4}\right)$$
$$+ \left(222 - \frac{28^2}{4}\right)$$

$$= 80.00$$

CHECK: 75.00 + 80.00 = 155.00

	SS	df	MS	F
Between Wars	75.00	3	25.00	3.75
Within Groups	80.00	12	6.67	
Total	155.00	15		

$F_{.05}$ (3,12) = 3.49. There are significant differences among the four groups of veterans. The HSD value required for statistical significance is 4.42 ($s_{\overline{X}}$ = 1.29). Only the comparison between WW II veterans and the hospitalized Viet Nam veterans is significant; HSD = 4.65. Hospitalized Viet Nam veterans gave significantly more guilt statements than WW II veterans.

3. $\Sigma X_{tot} = 49 + 74 + 78 + 83 = 284$

$\Sigma X^2_{tot} = 269 + 574 + 636 + 711 = 2190$

$$SS_{tot} = 2190 - \frac{284^2}{40} = 173.60$$

$$SS_{anesthetics} = \frac{49^2}{10} + \frac{74^2}{10} + \frac{78^2}{10} + \frac{83^2}{10} - \frac{284^2}{40}$$
$$= 68.60$$

$$SS_{wg} = (269 - \frac{49^2}{10}) + (574 - \frac{74^2}{10}) +$$
$$+ (636 - \frac{78^2}{10}) + (711 - \frac{83^2}{10})$$

$$= 28.90 + 26.40 + 27.60 + 22.10 = 105$$

CHECK: $173.60 = 68.60 + 105$

Source	df	SS	MS	F	p
Between Anesthetics	3	68.60	22.8667	7.84	< .01
Within Group	36	105.00	2.9267		
Total	39	173.60			

There are highly significant differences in well-being among the four groups of infants as measured by the Apgar Scale.

The $s_{\bar{X}}$ required for Tukey HSD tests is

$$\sqrt{\frac{2.917}{10}} = .540 \quad HSD_{.05} = 3.84$$

When the HSD tests are calculated, the Apgar scores of twilight neonates is significantly less than any of the other three methods. The other three methods do not differ significantly among themselves.

4.

Business Owners and Managers		Blue Collar Workers		Laborers	
X_1	$X_1{}^2$	X_2	$X_2{}^2$	X_3	$X_3{}^2$
18	324	18	324	15	225
17	289	16	256	14	196
16	256	15	225	14	196
16	256	15	225	13	169
15	225	14	196	13	169
14	196	14	196	12	144
14	196	12	144	11	121
13	169	11	121	10	100
9	81	9	81	8	64
		7	49	6	36
		6	36	4	16
		3	9	2	4
Σ = 132	1992	140	1862	122	1440

$$\overline{X}_1 = \frac{132}{9} = 14.6667 \qquad \overline{X}_2 = \frac{140}{12} = 11.6667$$

$$\overline{X}_3 = \frac{122}{12} = 10.1667$$

$$\Sigma X_{tot} = 132 + 140 + 122 = 394$$

$$\Sigma X^2{}_{tot} = 1992 + 1862 + 1440 = 5294$$

$$SS_{tot} = 5294 - \frac{394^2}{33} = 589.8788$$

$$SS_{citizens} = \frac{132^2}{9} + \frac{140^2}{12} + \frac{122^2}{12} - \frac{394^2}{33} = 105.5455$$

$$SS_{wg} = \left(1992 - \frac{132^2}{9}\right) + \left(1862 - \frac{140^2}{12}\right)$$
$$+ \left(1440 - \frac{122^2}{12}\right) = 484.3333$$

CHECK: $589.8788 = 105.5455 + 484.3333$

Source	df	SS	MS	F	p
Between					
Citizens	2	105.5455	52.7728	3.2688	> .05
Within	30	484.3333	16.1444		
Total	32	589.8788			

The F value barely misses significance at the .05 level ($F_{.05}$ = 3.32) so the null hypothesis must be retained. There is no

167

significant evidence that the three groups differ in their attitudes toward city government.

CHAPTER 10

Multiple-Choice Questions

1.	1	5.	1	9.	4	13.	3
2.	3	6.	3	10.	1	14.	4
3.	4	7.	3	11.	4		
4.	1	8.	1	12.	3		

Interpretation

1. The therapy was effective with both mobility groups, since significantly fewer instances of disorientation were reported for therapy patients in both wheelchair and mobile groups. Since the interaction effect was not significant, the effect of the therapy does not seem to depend on the mobility of the patients.

2. All effects are significant beyond the .01 level. Interpretation of the main effects, however, must be made in light of the significant interaction.

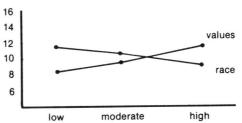

This interaction graph indicates that Rokeach is correct for those with low or moderate prejudice, i.e., prejudice is aroused more by perceived differences from oneself in values than in race. For high-prejudice people, however, the reverse is true. Racial differences arouse more prejudice than do differences in values.

168

3. The description of the physical attractiveness of the telephone personality did affect the rating given the person "as a person." This effect did not depend on the sex of the subject; it was true of both sexes. This can be seen from the interaction graph where the lines for both sexes drop as attractiveness decreases.

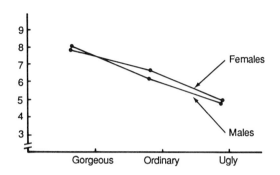

Mean Differences

	Gorgeous	Ordinary
Ordinary	1.75*	
Ugly	3.40**	1.65*

*p < .05, **p < .01

The last step in this analysis is to interpret the mean differences for the one main effect that was significant. All three of the pairwise comparisons of the variable, description, are significant. (The critical value was 1.36 for the .05 level [3.44 × .395 = 1.36] and 1.73 for the .01 level [4.37 × .395 = 1.73]. Note that N is 20 for these comparisons.) Thus, each physical description had an effect on the rating of the person in the conversation. Being described as "gorgeous" resulted in significantly higher ratings than either "ordinary" or "ugly." Being described as "ordinary" resulted in significantly higher ratings than being described as "ugly."

Problems

1. Attitude Toward Washing Dishes (Before Task)

	Low	High
	4	7
	3	6
Money	3	5
	2	5

$\Sigma X_{A_1B_1}$	12	$\Sigma X_{A_2B_1}$	23	ΣX_{B_1}	35
$\Sigma X^2_{A_1B_1}$	38	$\Sigma X^2_{A_2B_1}$	135	$\Sigma X^2_{B_1}$	173
$\bar{X}_{A_1B_1}$	3.00	$\bar{X}_{A_2B_1}$	5.75	$\bar{X}_{B_1}$	4.3750

	Low	High
	5	7
Thanks	3	6
	2	6
	1	5

$\Sigma X_{A_1B_2}$	11	$\Sigma X_{A_2B_2}$	24	ΣX_{B_2}	35
$\Sigma X^2_{A_1B_2}$	39	$\Sigma X^2_{A_2B_2}$	146	$\Sigma X^2_{B_2}$	185
$\bar{X}_{A_1B_2}$	2.75	$\bar{X}_{A_2B_2}$	6.00	$\bar{X}_{B_2}$	4.3750

ΣX_{A_1}	23	ΣX_{A_2}	47	ΣX_{tot}	70
$\Sigma X^2_{A_1}$	77	$\Sigma X^2_{A_2}$	281	ΣX^2_{tot}	358
$\bar{X}_{A_1}$	2.8750	$\bar{X}_{A_2}$	5.8750	$\bar{X}_{tot}$	4.3750

$$SS_{tot} = 358 - \frac{70^2}{16} = 358 - 306.25 = 51.75$$

$$SS_{bg} = \frac{12^2}{4} + \frac{23^2}{4} + \frac{11^2}{4} + \frac{24^2}{4} - \frac{70^2}{16}$$
$$= 36 + 132.25 + 30.25 + 144 - 306.25$$
$$= 36.25$$

$$SS_{attitudes} = \frac{23^2}{8} + \frac{47^2}{8} - \frac{70^2}{16}$$
$$= 66.1250 + 276.1250 - 306.25$$
$$= 36$$

$$SS_{rewards} = \frac{35^2}{8} + \frac{35^2}{8} - \frac{70^2}{16}$$
$$= 153.1250 + 153.1250 - 306.25$$
$$= 0$$

170

$$SS_{AB} = 4[(3.00 - 2.8750 - 4.3750 + 4.3750)^2$$
$$+ (2.75 - 4.3750 - 2.875 + 4.3750)^2$$
$$+ (5.75 - 4.3750 - 5.875 + 4.3750)^2$$
$$+ (6.00 - 4.3750 - 5.8750 + 4.3750)^2]$$
$$= 4[(.1250)^2 + (.125)^2 + (.125)^2$$
$$+ (.125)^2]$$
$$= 4(.0156 + .0156 + .0156 + .0156)$$
$$= 24.96$$

CHECK:

$$SS_{AB} = 36.25 - 36 - 0 = .25$$

$$SS_{wg} = (38 - \frac{12^2}{4}) + (135 - \frac{23^2}{4})$$
$$+ (39 - \frac{11^2}{4}) + (146 - \frac{24^2}{4})$$
$$= 2.00 + 2.75 + 8.75 + 2.00 = 15.50$$

CHECK:

$$SS_{tot} = 51.75 = 36.25 + 15.50$$

Source	df	SS	MS	F	p
Attitudes (A)	1	36.00	36.00	27.87	< .01
Rewards (B)	1	0	0	0.00	> .05
AB	1	.25	.25	0.19	> .05
Within Groups	12	15.50	1.2917		
Total	15				

The only significant effect is for Factor A, Attitudes. Since the factor has only two levels, no comparison test is needed-- simply examine the means. Clearly, those with high attitudes toward washing dishes before the task still had higher attitudes afterward than those whose beginning attitudes were low. The attitudinal difference between the groups remained regardless of the reward used. There is no evidence here to support McCuller's assertion. Perhaps you would like to actually do the study to see what would really happen. You would at least gain a lot of clean dishes.

2. $SS_{tot} = 6299 - \frac{363^2}{24} = 6299 - 5490.3750$
$= 808.6250$

$SS_{bg} = \frac{62^2}{6} + \frac{123^2}{6} + \frac{114^2}{6} + \frac{62^2}{6} - \frac{363^2}{24}$
$= 682.6667 + 2521.50 + 2166$
$+ 640.6667 - 5490.3750$
$= 520.4584$

$SS_{education} = \frac{178^2}{12} + \frac{185^2}{12} - \frac{363^2}{12}$
$= 2640.3333 + 2852.0833$
$- 5490.3750$
$= 2.0416$

$SS_{arguments} = \frac{187^2}{12} + \frac{176^2}{12} - \frac{363^2}{24}$
$= 2914.0833 + 2581.3333$
$- 5490.3750$
$= 5.0416$

$SS_{AB} = 6[(10.667 - 14.8333 - 15.5833$
$+ 15.1250)^2 + (20.50 - 15.4167$
$- 15.5833 + 15.1250)^2 + (19.00$
$- 14.8333 - 14.6667 + 15.1250)^2$
$+ (10.3333 - 15.4167 - 14.6667$
$+ 15.1250)^2]$
$= 6[(-4.6249)^2 + (4.6250)^2$
$+ (4.6250)^2 - (-4.6251)^2]$
$= 6(21.3810 + 21.3906 + 21.3906$
$+ 21.3916) = 513.3228$

CHECK:

$$SS_{AB} = 520.4584 - 2.0416 - 5.0416$$
$$= 513.3752 \text{ (within rounding error)}$$

$$SS_{wg} = (808 - \frac{64^2}{6}) + (2603 - \frac{123^2}{6})$$
$$+ (2218 - \frac{114^2}{6}) + (670 - \frac{62^2}{6})$$
$$= 125.3333 + 81.50 + 52.00 + 29.3333$$
$$= 288.1667$$

CHECK:
$$SS_{tot} = 808.6250 = 520.4584 + 288.1667$$

Source	df	SS	MS	F	p
Education (A)	1	2.0416	2.0416	<1.0	>.05
Arguments (B)	1	5.0416	5.0416	<1.0	>.05
AB	1	513.3228	513.3228	35.63	<.01
Within Groups	20	288.1667	14.4083		
Total	23	808.6250			

Neither main effect was significant, indicating that neither educational level nor type of argument influenced attitude change. The significant interaction effect, however, tells a different story as can be seen from the interaction graph.

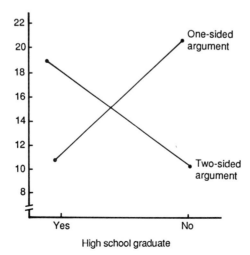

173

Clearly, both variables influenced attitude change, but the effect of each variable was dependent upon the other. The one-sided argument was effective only for nongraduates, whereas the two-sided argument was effective only for graduates of high school.

3. $SS_{tot} = 1234 - \dfrac{210^2}{54} = 1234 - 816.6667$

   $= 417.3333$

   $SS_{bg} = \dfrac{15^2}{6} + \dfrac{11^2}{6} + \dfrac{43^2}{6} + \dfrac{16^2}{6} + \dfrac{11^2}{6} + \dfrac{46^2}{6}$
   $+ \dfrac{15^2}{6} + \dfrac{10^2}{6} + \dfrac{43^2}{6} - \dfrac{210^2}{54}$

   $= 37.50 + 20.1667 + 308.1667 +$

   $\quad + 42.6667 + 20.1667 + 352.6667$

   $\quad + 37.50 + 16.6667 + 308.1667$

   $\quad - 816.6667$

   $= 327.0002$

   $SS_{information} = \dfrac{46^2}{18} + \dfrac{32^2}{18} + \dfrac{132^2}{18} - \dfrac{210^2}{54}$

   $\quad = 117.5556 + 56.8889 + 968.00$

   $\quad - 816.6667$

   $\quad = 325.7778$

   $SS_{diagnosticians} = \dfrac{69^2}{18} + \dfrac{73^2}{18} + \dfrac{68^2}{18} + \dfrac{210^2}{54}$

   $\quad = 264.50 + 296.0556$

   $\quad + 256.8889 - 816.6667$

   $\quad = .7778$

$SS_{AB} = 6[(2.50) - 2.5556 - 3.3833$

   $+ 3.8889)^2 + (2.6667 - 2.5556$

   $- 4.0555 + 3.8889)^2 + (2.50$

   $- 2.5556 - 3.7778 + 3.8889)^2$

   $+ (1.8333 - 1.7778 - 3.8883$

   $+ 3.8889)^2 + (1.8333 - 1.7778$

$$- 4.0555 + 3.8889)^2 + (1.6667$$
$$- 1.7778 - 3.7778 + 3.8889)^2$$
$$+ (7.1667 - 7.3333 - 3.8333$$
$$+ 3.8889)^2 + (7.6667 - 7.3333$$
$$- 4.0555 + 3.8889)^2 + (7.1667$$
$$- 7.2222 - 2.7778 + 3.8889)^2$$
$$= 6(0)^2 + (-.0555)^2 + (.0555)^2$$
$$+ (.0561)^2 + (-.1111)^2 + (0)^2$$
$$+ (-.1111)^2 + (.1668)^2 + (-.0555)^2$$
$$= 6(0) + .0031 + .0031 + .0031$$
$$+ .0123 + .0123 + .0278 + .0031$$
$$= .3888$$

CHECK: $327.0002 - 325.7778 - .7778 = .4444$

$$SS_{wg} = (43 - \frac{15^2}{6}) + (56 - \frac{16^2}{6}) + (47 - \frac{15^2}{6})$$
$$+ (23 - \frac{11^2}{6}) + (25 - \frac{11^2}{6})$$
$$+ (20 - \frac{10^2}{6}) + (329 - \frac{43^2}{6})$$
$$+ (360 - \frac{46^2}{6}) + (331 - \frac{43^2}{6})$$
$$= 5.50 + 13.3333 + 9.50 + 2.8333$$
$$+ 4.8333 + 3.3333 + 20.8333$$
$$+ 7.3333 + 22.8333$$
$$= 90.3331$$

CHECK: $417.3333 = 327.0002 + 90.3331$

Source	df	SS	MS	F	p
Informa-tion (A)	2	325.7778	162.8889	81.1442	<.01
Diagnos-ticians (B)	2	.7778	.3889	0.19	>.05
AB	4	.4444	.1111	0.06	>.05
Within Groups	45	90.3331	2.0074		
Total	53	417.3331			

The information given the diagnosticians did have an effect on the evaluation they made of the man in the interview (Factor A). There were no significant differences among the clinical psychologists, psychiatrists, and graduate students in their evaluation of the man (Factor B). The effect of the kind of information given did not depend upon whether the evaluations were made by clinical psychologists, psychiatrists, or graduate students (AB Interaction).

The critical value required for a difference between the information means to be significant at the .05 level is 1.15; for the .01 level the critical value is 1.46. ($s_{\overline{X}} = \sqrt{\frac{2.007}{18}} = .334$; $HSD_{.05} = 3.44$; $HSD_{.01} = 4.37$.) The differences between group means are shown in the table.

Mean Differences

	Employment	Normal
Normal	.778	
Psychotic	4.777**	5.555**

**$p < .01$

Clinical psychologists, psychiatrists, and graduate students are about equally influenced by a person's label when they are watching a taped interview. If the person is labeled "psychotic" all three groups rate the person as being significantly more severely disturbed than if the person is labeled "normal" or as an "applicant" for employment. There is no significant difference in the "normal" and "applicant" labels.

CHAPTER 11

Multiple-Choice Questions

1. 3	5. 1	9. 1	13. 2
2. 3	6. 2	10. 4	
3. 1	7. 2	11. 2	
4. 1	8. 3	12. 1	

Interpretation

1. Since $\chi^2_{.001}$ (1 df) = 10.83, the null
    hypothesis can be rejected; the two vari-
    ables are not independent. Those with
    greater than five years of experience tend
    to be lumpers; those with less experience
    tend to be splitters.

2. This is a goodness-of-fit problem that asks
    whether this year's frequencies fit predic-
    tions based on previous years. Thus, we
    would expect this year's 1191 applications
    to be distributed in the following way:

    1. Five-county area: 51% of 1191 = 607.4

    2. Rest of state: 40% of 1191 = 476.4

    3. Out of state: 9% of 1191 = 107.2

    $\chi^2_{.001}$ (2 df) = 13.82. Reject the null
    hypothesis, and conclude that the campaign
    was quite successful in attracting out-of-
    state requests for applications. Note that
    the expected frequencies of the "five-
    county" area and the "rest of state" cate-
    gories are less than expected. This is a
    necessary consequence of the $\Sigma O = \Sigma E$ rule.
    The question of the absolute increase or
    decrease in applications is not addressed
    in this problem.

3. χ^2 for 1 df at α = .05 is 3.84. There is a
    significant difference in the number of
    decisions won by husband and wife in the
    two cultures. The wife is more likely to

win out in disagreements in the Navaho culture and the husband more likely to win in
the Mormon culture.

Problems

1. $\chi^2 = \dfrac{32[(10)(12) - (8)(2)]^2}{(18)(14)(12)(20)} = 5.72$

$\chi^2_{.05}$ (1 df) = 3.84. Therefore, reject the
null hypothesis and conclude that living
conditions make a difference in survival
rates. Those that were isolated were more
likely to be alive than those that lived
together.

2. The expected frequencies are:

$\dfrac{9}{16}(186) = 104.63;\quad \dfrac{3}{16}(186) = 34.88$

$\dfrac{1}{16}(186) = 11.63$

O	E	O-E	$(O-E)^2$	$\dfrac{(O-E)^2}{E}$
90	104.63	-14.63	214.04	2.05
39	34.88	4.12	16.97	.49
39	34.88	4.12	16.97	.49
18	11.63	6.38	40.64	3.50
				$\chi^2 = 6.53$

$\chi^2_{.05}$ (3 df) = 7.82. Thus, retain the null
hypothesis and conclude that a 9:3:3:1
model is an adequate fit for these data.

3.

	College Educated	High School Dropouts	Σ
S.A.	2	4	6
M.A.	7	10	17
S.A.	15	24	39
N.	19	21	40
S.D.	23	18	41
M.D.	12	9	21
S.D.	6	3	9
Σ	84	89	173

Expected Frequencies:

$$\frac{(6)(84)}{173} = 2.9133 \qquad \frac{(6)(89)}{173} = 3.0867$$

$$\frac{(17)(84)}{173} = 8.2543 \qquad \frac{(17)(89)}{173} = 8.7457$$

$$\frac{(39)(84)}{173} = 18.9364 \qquad \frac{(39)(89)}{173} = 20.0636$$

$$\frac{(40)(84)}{173} = 19.4220 \qquad \frac{(40)(89)}{173} = 20.5780$$

$$\frac{(41)(84)}{173} = 19.9075 \qquad \frac{(41)(89)}{173} = 21.0925$$

$$\frac{(21)(84)}{173} = 10.1965 \qquad \frac{(21)(89)}{173} = 10.8035$$

$$\frac{(9)(84)}{173} = 4.3699 \qquad \frac{(9)(89)}{173} = 4.6301$$

Since the four extreme categories have expected frequencies less than 5, it is necessary to combine the "strong" and "moderate" categories and recompute frequencies for them. The table now looks like this:

	College Educated	High School Dropouts	Σ
Strong and Moderate Agreement	9	14	23
Slight Agreement	14	24	39
Neutral	19	21	40
Slight Disagreement	23	18	41
Moderate and Strong Disagreement	18	12	30
Σ	84	89	173

The new expected frequencies are:

$$\frac{(23)(84)}{173} = 11.1676 \qquad \frac{(23)(89)}{173} = 11.8324$$

$$\frac{(30)(84)}{173} = 14.5665 \qquad \frac{(30)(89)}{173} = 15.4335$$

The other expected frequencies are unchanged.

O	E	O-E	$(O-E)^2$	$\dfrac{(O-E)^2}{E}$
9	11.1676	-2.1676	4.6985	.4207
15	18.9364	-3.9364	15.4952	.8183
19	19.4220	- .4220	.1781	.0092
23	19.9075	3.0925	9.5636	.4804
18	14.5665	3.4335	11.7890	.8093
14	11.8324	2.1676	4.6985	.3971
24	20.0636	3.9364	15.4950	.7723
21	20.5780	.4220	.1781	.0087
18	21.0925	-3.0925	9.5636	.4534
12	15.4335	-3.4335	11.7890	.7639

$$\chi^2 = 4.9333$$

The df for this problem is $(R - 1)(C - 1)$ with categories combined. $(7 - 1)(2 - 1) = 6$. The required χ^2 for the .05 level is 12.59. A χ^2 of 4.93 does not permit us to say that there is any relationship between education and degree of agreement or dis-agreement with the statement.

4.

	O	E	O-E	$(O-E)^2$	$\dfrac{(O-E)^2}{E}$
up to 4500 pounds	155	143.82	-11.18	124.99	.869
4501- 6000	82	91.80	9.80	96.04	1.046
6001- 10,000	37	45.90	8.90	79.21	1.726
10,000 up	32	24.48	-7.52	56.55	2.310

$$\chi^2 = 5.951$$

$\chi^2_{.05}$ (3 df) = 7.82. The obtained chi square is not significant. The data fit the predictions made by the engineer according to this goodness-of-fit test.

CHAPTER 12

Multiple Choice

1.	3	5.	1	9.	2	13.	2
2.	1	6.	4	10.	5 (6.5)	14.	3
3.	2	7.	2	11.	2		
4.	2	8.	2	12.	1		

Interpretation

1. A.   Mann-Whitney U test
   B.   Spearman's r_s
   C.   Wilcoxon matched-pairs signed-ranks
        t test
   D.   Mann-Whitney U test
   E.   Wilcoxon-Wilcox multiple-comparisons
        test
   F.   Wilcoxon matched-pairs signed-ranks
        t test

2. A Wilcoxon-Wilcox multiple-comparisons
   test is appropriate.

	0 (73)	20 (54)	40 (44.5)	60 (27.5)
20(54)	19			
40(44.5)	28.5	9.5		
60(27.5)	45.5	26.5	17	
80(11)	62**	43	33.5	16.5

   $^*p < .05$
   $^{**}p < .01$

   The conclusion from these data (and
   from Gates' and many others) is that self-
   recitation improves recall. The trend in
   the data is steadily upward; the more self-
   recitation, the better the recall.

3. With N = 9, a t value of 5.0 or less is
   required for significance at α = .05.
   Since this t = 5.5, the hypothesis that the

difference between the before and after scores is due to chance cannot be rejected.

4. You can see from the second page of Table H in the boldface type (α = .05, two-tailed test), for N_1 = 14, N_2 = 9, that a U value of 31 or less is required for significance. Thus, those who had a sex education course were significantly less sexually active than those who had not had such a course. Not only does this argument against sex education appear to be wrong--its reverse seems to be true.

5. Pilot competency is more highly correlated with general knowledge than it is with a task that has components similar to those used by pilots. Two comments are in order. Flying an airplane well has a heavy cognitive component to it and the correlations among any two motor skills are uniformly low.

Problems

1.

Time on Target (T.O.T.) in Seconds	Pilot Competency Score	T.O.T. Rank	Pilot Score Rank	R	R^2
18	37	4	7	-3	9
15	57	6	2	4	16
28	63	1	1	0	0
25	41	2	6	-4	16
9	31	8	8	0	0
17	51	5	3	2	4
23	42	3	5	-2	4
11	45	7	4	3	9
				Σ =	58

$$r_s = 1 - \frac{6\Sigma D^2}{N(N^2-1)} = 1 - \frac{6(58)}{8(63)} = .31$$

182

2.

Rank of Supervisor	Training Program
1	yes
2	no
3	no
4	yes
5	yes
6	yes
7	no
8	no

Let Group 1 be Yes.

$\Sigma_{yes} = 1 + 4 + 5 + 6 = 16$

$\Sigma_{no} = 2 + 3 + 7 + 8 = 20$

For the Yes group,

$$U = (N_1)(N_2) + \frac{N_1(N_1+1)}{2} - \Sigma R_1$$

$$= (4)(4) + \frac{(4)(5)}{2} - 16 = 10$$

For the No group,

$$U = (N_1)(N_2) + \frac{N_2(N_2+1)}{2} - \Sigma R_2$$

$$= (4)(4) + \frac{(4)(5)}{2} - 20 = 6$$

This is a one-tailed test since interest is only in whether the training improves ratings by employees. The company certainly would not buy the program if it lowered ratings.

Now, enter Table H with the smaller U value of 6.

With $N_1 = 4$ and $N_2 = 4$, a U of 1 or less is required for rejection of the null hypothesis. The company should not buy the training program without better evidence of its effectiveness.

3.

Matched Pairs	Attitude Scores Untrained	Trained	D	Signed Ranks
1	21	23	-2	-3
2	12	18	-6	-6
3	17	22	-5	-5
4	23	23	0	elim.
5	16	17	-1	-1.5
6	21	24	-3	-4
7	19	27	-8	-7
8	14	13	1	1.5

$\Sigma_{positive} = 1.5$

$\Sigma_{negative} = -26.5$

$t = 1.5$

$N = 7$

For a two-tailed test, Table J shows that a
t of 2.0 or less is required for significance at $\alpha = .05$. Since $1.5 < 2.0$, the
hypothesis of no difference between trained
and untrained nurses may be rejected.
Scores of those trained are higher, so the
conclusion is that attitudes are more positive after the training. The program appears to be effective in improving
attitudes toward patients with psychological problems.

4.

Chain A		Chain B		Chain C		Chain D	
X	Rank	X	Rank	X	Rank	X	Rank
38	12	29	4	41	15	50	24
26	1	31	5	47	21	45	19
44	18	34	8	39	13	33	7
35	9	40	14	43	17	48	22
37	11	27	2	36	10	32	6
46	20	28	3	42	16	49	23
Σ (ranks) 71		36		92		101	

	A(71)	B(36)	C(92)
B(36)	35		
C(92)	21	56	
D(101)	30	65*	9

184

The critical difference from Table K for
$N = 6$ and $K = 4$ is 62.9 at $\alpha = .05$. The
only difference this great is the difference between Chain B and Chain D. You can
say that Chain D has cleaner supermarkets
than Chain B. The next question is "Should
you?" This question refers back to the
material in Chapter 7 on significance and
importance. Notice that scores could range
from 1 to 50 but that the lowest score made
was 26. How dirty must a supermarket be to
affect the food? Will a little dust on the
floor or on the shelf affect the contents
of a can of peas or a box of cereal?
Again, statistical significance and importance are not synonymous.

APPENDIX: ARITHMETIC AND ALGEBRA REVIEW

PROBLEMS

1.	15.844	2.	205.535
3.	34.657	4.	26.94
5.	373.817	6.	.612
7.	65.28	8.	.038
9.	10.64	10.	64.763
11.	.026	12.	9.701
13.	5.246	14.	10.909
15.	18.25	16.	.496

17. $.50 + .25 + .125 = .875$

18. $.6667 + .75 = 1.417$

19. $.8571 + .625 + .9048 = 2.387$

20. $.8 + .2222 = 1.022$

21. $.375 - .2 = .175$

22. $.6957 - .8462 = -.151$

23. $.2 - .125 = .075$

24. $.6667 - .8889 = -.222$

25. $.6667 \times .5714 = .381$

26. $.8 \times .3333 = .267$

27. $.7 \times .5 \times .6667 = .233$

28. $.75 \times .3333 \times .375 = .094$

29. $.5 \div .3333 = 1.500$

30. $.75 \div .5 = 1.5$

31. $.6316 \div .8571 = .737$

32. $25 \div .5 = 50$

33.	1	34.	-40
35.	-55	36.	22
37.	-3	38.	28
39.	-2	40.	421
41.	10	42.	-24
43.	140	44.	-147
45.	2	46.	-2.667
47.	-2.167	48.	.714

49. $\frac{15}{27} = .556$

50. $\frac{10}{27} \times 100 = 37.037\%$

51. $.22 \times 27 = 5.94$ or 6

52.	10 - 6 = 4	53.	11
54.	4	55.	2
56.	40	57.	-8, 28
58.	45.5, 58.5	59.	-11.25, -4.75
60.	-.03, .67	61.	36
62.	5.664	63.	342.25

64. .000081   This is a case where good judgment suggests that you carry more decimal places than the instructions indicate.

Complex Problems

65. $\frac{19}{3} = 6.3333$

66. $\frac{(1)^2 + (3)^2}{4(8)} = \frac{1 + 9}{32} = \frac{10}{32} = .313$

67. $\frac{(66 - 14.4) + (75 - 12.8)}{9} = \frac{51.6 + 62.2}{9}$

$= \frac{113.8}{9} = 12.644$

68. $\frac{100 - 90}{\sqrt{(190 - 150)(110 - 93)}} = \frac{10}{\sqrt{(40)(17)}} = \frac{10}{\sqrt{680}}$

$= \frac{10}{26.0768}$

69. $\dfrac{25 - 72}{53.55} = \dfrac{-47}{53.55} = -.878$

70. $36 - (1.96)\left(\dfrac{2}{10}\right) = 36 - (1.96)(.2)$

$= 36 - .392 = 35.608$

71. $\dfrac{-6.8}{\sqrt{\dfrac{73}{9}(.1667 + .3333)}} = \dfrac{-6.8}{\sqrt{(8.111)(.5)}}$

$= \dfrac{-6.8}{\sqrt{4.0556}} = \dfrac{-6.8}{2.0138} = -3.3767$

72. $\sqrt{\dfrac{21 - 10.6667}{6}} = \sqrt{\dfrac{10.3333}{6}} = \sqrt{1.7222} = 1.312$

73. $\sqrt{\dfrac{(68 - 12.5) + (54 - 24.2)}{42}} = \sqrt{\dfrac{55.5 + 29.8}{42}}$

$= \sqrt{\dfrac{85.3}{42}} = \sqrt{2.031} = 1.425$

74. $\dfrac{\left(14 - \dfrac{157}{16}\right)^2}{1.6575 + .8288} = \dfrac{(14 - 9.8125)^2}{2.4863}$

$= \dfrac{(4.1875)^2}{2.4863} = \dfrac{17.5352}{2.4863} = 7.053$

75. $x + 5 = (3)(4.25)$

$x = 12.75 - 5$

$x = 7.75$

76. $24 - 8 = 6.42x$

$\dfrac{16}{6.42} = x$

$2.492 = x$

77. $\dfrac{8}{4} = 2x - 2$

$2 + 2 = 2x$

$\dfrac{4}{2} = x$

$2 = x$

78.

$$3 = \frac{3x + 5}{2}$$

$$(2)(3) = 3x + 5$$

$$6 - 5 = 3x$$

$$\frac{1}{3} = x$$

$$.333 = x$$

REFERENCES

Aronson, E., & Mills, J. (1959). The effect of severity of initiation on liking for a group. Journal of Abnormal and Social Psychology, 59, 177-181.

Calhoun, J.P., & Johnston, J.O. (1968). Manifest anxiety and visual acuity. Perceptual and Motor Skills, 27, 1177-1178.

Cohen, I.B. (March, 1984). Florence Nightingale. Scientific American, 250, 128-137.

D'Agnostino, R.B. (1973). How much does a 40-pound box of bananas weigh? In F. Mosteller et al., Statistics by example: Detecting patterns. Reading, MA: Addison-Wesley.

Gates, A.I. (1917). Recitation as a factor in memorizing. New York Archives of Psychology, No. 40.

Hovland, C., Lumsdaine, A., & Sheffield, F. (1949). Experiments on mass communication. Princeton, NJ: Princeton University Press.

Hulse, S.H. (1973). Patterned reinforcement. In G.H. Bower (Ed.), The psychology of learning and motivation, Vol. 7, New York: Academic Press.

Koonce, J.M., Chambliss, D.J., & Irion, A.L. (1964). Long-term reminiscence in the pursuit-rotor habit. Journal of Experimental Psychology, 67, 498-500.

Lazarus, R.S., & Alfert, E. (1964). Shortcircuiting of threat by experimentally altering cognitive and social appraisal. Journal of Abnormal and Social Psychology, 69, 195-205.

Luchins, A.S. (1942). Mechanization in problem solving: The effect of einstellung. Psychology Monographs, 54, No. 6.

Miller, N.E., & Bugelski, R. (1948). Minor studies of aggression II: The influence of frustrations imposed by the in-group on attitudes expressed toward out-groups. Journal of Psychology, 25, 437-442.

Mishara, B., & Kastenbaum, R. (1980). Alcohol and old age. New York: Grune and Stratton.

Spatz, C., & Jones. S.D. (1971). Starvation anorexia as an explanation of "self-starvation" of rats living in activity wheels. Journal of Comparative and Physiological Psychology, 77, 313-317.

Statistical abstract of the United States: 1987 (107th ed.). (1986). Washington, DC: US Bureau of the Census.

Stodtbeck, F. (1951). Husband-wife interaction over revealed differences. American Sociological Review, 16, 468-473.

Taylor, W.F., & Hoedt, K.C. (1966). The effects of praise upon the quality and quantity of creative writing. Journal of Educational Research, 60, 80-83.

Temerlin, M.K. (1968). Suggestion effects in psychotic diagnosis. Journal of Nervous and Mental Disorders, 147, 349-353.

Turnbull, C.M. (1961). The forest people. New York: Simon and Schuster.

Van Cott, H.P., & Kinkade, R.G. (Eds.) (1972). Human engineering guide to equipment design (Rev. ed.). Joint Army-Navy-Air Force Steering Committee, Washington, D.C.: U.S. Government Printing Office.

Warden, C.J. (1931). Animal motivation studies: The albino rat. Columbia University Press.

Wender, P.H., & Klein, D.F. (1981). The promise of biological psychiatry, Psychology Today, 15(2), 25-41.

MAI

APR 23, 2011   7/17/95